Copenhagen

Michael Frayn was born in 1933 in the suburbs of London. He began his career as a reporter on the *Guardian*, and became a columnist, first for the *Guardian*, then for the *Observer*. A selection of his columns, first published in four volumes, appeared as *The Original Michael Frayn*, and his latest volume, *Speak After the Beep*, a collection of recent *Guardian* articles, was published in November 1995. He has written eight novels: *The Tin Men, The Russian Interpreter, Towards the End of the Morning, A Very Private Life, Sweet Dreams, The Trick of It, A Landing on the Sun* and *Now You Know*, together with a volume of philosophy, *Constructions*. He has also written screenplays for the cinema and TV: *Clockwise, First and Last* and *Remember Me?* as well as numerous stage plays including: *Alphabetical Order, Donkeys' Years, Clouds, Make and Break, Noises Off, Benefactors, Look Look, Here* and *Now You Know*. He has translated Chekhov's last four plays, dramatised a selection of his one-act plays and short stories under the title of *The Sneeze*, and adapted his first, untitled play, as *Wild Honey*. He has also translated one modern Russian play – Yuri Trifonov's *Exchange*.

Copenhagen

Michael Frayn

Methuen Drama

Published by Methuen

4 6 8 10 9 7 5

Copyright © 1998 by Michael Frayn
Michael Frayn has asserted his right under the Copyright, Designs and Patents
Act, 1988 to be identified as the author of this work.

First published in the United Kingdom in 1998 by Methuen Drama,
Random House, 20 Vauxhall Bridge Road, London SW1V 2SA

Random House Australia (Pty) Limited
20 Alfred Street, Milsons Point, Sydney,
New South Wales 2061, Australia

Random House New Zealand Limited
18 Poland Road, Glenfield,
Auckland 10, New Zealand

Random House South Africa (Pty) Limited
Endulini, 5A Jubilee Road, Parktown 2193, South Africa

Random House UK Limited Reg. No. 954009

A CIP catalogue record for this book
is available from the British Library

ISBN 0 413 72490 5

Typeset by Deltatype Ltd, Birkenhead, Merseyside
Printed and bound in Great Britain by
Mackays of Chatham plc, Chatham, Kent

Caution

Copenhagen

Copenhagen was first performed at the Cottesloe Theatre, Royal National Theatre, London on 21 May 1998 with the following cast:

Margrethe   Sara Kestelman
Bohr   David Burke
Heisenberg   Matthew Marsh

Directed by Michael Blakemore
Designed by Peter J. Davison
Lighting by Mark Henderson
Sound by Simon Baker

Author's note
I should like to record my gratitude to Professor Balázs L. Gyorffy, Professor of Physics at Bristol University, for his kindness in reading the text of the play and making a number of corrections and suggestions.

Michael Frayn, 1998

Act One

Margrethe But why?

Bohr You're still thinking about it?

Margrethe Why did he come to Copenhagen?

Bohr Does it matter, my love, now we're all three of us dead and gone?

Margrethe Some questions remain long after their owners have died. Lingering like ghosts. Looking for the answers they never found in life.

Bohr Some questions have no answers to find.

Margrethe Why did he come? What was he trying to tell you?

Bohr He did explain later.

Margrethe He explained over and over again. Each time he explained it became more obscure.

Bohr It was probably very simple, when you come right down to it: he wanted to have a talk.

Margrethe A talk? To the enemy? In the middle of a war?

Bohr Margrethe, my love, we were scarcely the enemy.

Margrethe It was 1941!

Bohr Heisenberg was one of our oldest friends.

Margrethe Heisenberg was German. We were Danes. We were under German occupation.

Bohr It put us in a difficult position, certainly.

Margrethe I've never seen you as angry with anyone as you were with Heisenberg that night.

Bohr Not to disagree, but I believe I remained

remarkably calm.

Margrethe   I know when you're angry.

Bohr   It was as difficult for him as it was for us.

Margrethe   So why did he do it? Now no one can be hurt, now no one can be betrayed.

Bohr   I doubt if he ever really knew himself.

Margrethe   And he wasn't a friend. Not after that visit. That was the end of the famous friendship between Niels Bohr and Werner Heisenberg.

Heisenberg   Now we're all dead and gone, yes, and there are only two things the world remembers about me. One is the uncertainty principle, and the other is my mysterious visit to Niels Bohr in Copenhagen in 1941. Everyone understands uncertainty. Or thinks he does. No one understands my trip to Copenhagen. Time and time again I've explained it. To Bohr himself, and Margrethe. To interrogators and intelligence officers, to journalists and historians. The more I've explained, the deeper the uncertainty has become. Well, I shall be happy to make one more attempt. Now we're all dead and gone. Now no one can be hurt, now no one can be betrayed.

Margrethe   I never entirely liked him, you know. Perhaps I can say that to you now.

Bohr   Yes, you did. When he was first here in the twenties? Of course you did. On the beach at Tisvilde with us and the boys? He was one of the family.

Margrethe   Something alien about him, even then.

Bohr   So quick and eager.

Margrethe   Too quick. Too eager.

Bohr   Those bright watchful eyes.

Margrethe   Too bright. Too watchful.

Bohr   Well, he was a very great physicist. I never

changed my mind about that.

Margrethe They were all good, all the people who came to Copenhagen to work with you. You had most of the great pioneers in atomic theory here at one time or another.

Bohr And the more I look back on it, the more I think Heisenberg was the greatest of them all.

Heisenberg So what was Bohr? He was the first of us all, the father of us all. Modern atomic physics began when Bohr realised that quantum theory applied to matter as well as to energy. 1913. Everything we did was based on that great insight of his.

Bohr When you think that he first came here as my assistant in 1924 . . .

Heisenberg I'd only just finished my doctorate, and Bohr was the most famous atomic physicist in the world.

Bohr . . . and in just over a year he'd invented quantum mechanics.

Margrethe It came out of his work with you.

Bohr Within three he'd got uncertainty.

Margrethe And you'd done complementarity.

Bohr We argued them both out together.

Heisenberg We did most of our best work together.

Bohr Heisenberg usually led the way.

Heisenberg Bohr made sense of it all.

Bohr We operated like a business.

Heisenberg Chairman and managing director.

Margrethe Father and son.

Heisenberg A family business.

Margrethe Even though we had sons of our own.

Bohr   And we went on working together long after he ceased to be my assistant.

Heisenberg   Long after I'd left Copenhagen in 1927 and gone back to Germany. Long after I had a chair and a family of my own.

Margrethe   Then the Nazis came to power. . . .

Bohr   And it got more and more difficult. When the war broke out – impossible. Until that day in 1941.

Margrethe   When it finished forever.

Bohr   Yes, why did he do it?

Heisenberg   September, 1941. For years I had it down in my memory as October.

Margrethe   September. The end of September.

Bohr   A curious sort of diary memory is.

Heisenberg   You open the pages, and all the neat headings and tidy jottings dissolve around you.

Bohr   You step through the pages into the months and days themselves.

Margrethe   The past becomes the present inside your head.

Heisenberg   September, 1941, Copenhagen. . . . And at once – here I am, getting off the night train from Berlin with my colleague Carl von Weizsäcker. Two plain civilian suits and raincoats among all the field-grey Wehrmacht uniforms arriving with us, all the naval gold braid, all the well-tailored black of the SS. In my bag I have the text of the lecture I'm giving. In my head is another communication that has to be delivered. The lecture is on astrophysics. The text inside my head is a more difficult one.

Bohr   We obviously can't go to the lecture.

Margrethe   Not if he's giving it at the German Cultural

Institute – it's a Nazi propaganda organisation.

Bohr   He must know what we feel about that.

Heisenberg   Weizsäcker has been my John the Baptist, and written to warn Bohr of my arrival.

Margrethe   He wants to see you?

Bohr   I assume that's why he's come.

Heisenberg   But how can the actual meeting with Bohr be arranged?

Margrethe   He must have something remarkably important to say.

Heisenberg   It has to seem natural. It has to be private.

Margrethe   You're not really thinking of inviting him to the house?

Bohr   That's obviously what he's hoping.

Margrethe   Niels! They've occupied our country!

Bohr   He is not they.

Margrethe   He's one of them.

Heisenberg   First of all there's an official visit to Bohr's workplace, the Institute for Theoretical Physics, with an awkward lunch in the old familiar canteen. No chance to talk to Bohr, of course. Is he even present? There's Rozental . . . Petersen, I think . . . Christian Møller, almost certainly. . . . It's like being in a dream. You can never quite focus the precise details of the scene around you. At the head of the table – is that Bohr? I turn to look, and it's Bohr, it's Rozental, it's Møller, it's whoever I appoint to be there. . . . A difficult occasion, though – I remember that clearly enough.

Bohr   It was a disaster. He made a very bad impression. Occupation of Denmark unfortunate. Occupation of Poland, however, perfectly acceptable. Germany now certain to win the war.

Heisenberg Our tanks are almost at Moscow. What can stop us? Well, one thing, perhaps. One thing.

Bohr He knows he's being watched, of course. One must remember that. He has to be careful about what he says.

Margrethe Or he won't be allowed to travel abroad again.

Bohr My love, the Gestapo planted microphones in his house. He told Goudsmit when he was in America. The SS brought him in for interrogation in the basement at the Prinz-Albert-Strasse.

Margrethe And then they let him go again.

Heisenberg I wonder if they suspect for one moment how painful it was to get permission for this trip. The humiliating appeals to the Party, the demeaning efforts to have strings pulled by our friends in the Foreign Office.

Margrethe How did he seem? Is he greatly changed?

Bohr A little older.

Margrethe I still think of him as a boy.

Bohr He's nearly forty. A middle-aged professor, fast catching up with the rest of us.

Margrethe You still want to invite him here?

Bohr Let's add up the arguments on either side in a reasonably scientific way. Firstly, Heisenberg is a friend. . . .

Margrethe Firstly, Heisenberg is a German.

Bohr A White Jew. That's what the Nazis called him. He taught so-called Jewish physics. And refused to stop. He stuck with Einstein and relativity, in spite of the most terrible attacks.

Margrethe All the real Jews have lost their jobs. He's still teaching.

Bohr He's still teaching relativity.

Margrethe Still a professor at Leipzig.

Bohr At Leipzig, yes. Not at Munich. They kept him out of the chair at Munich.

Margrethe He could have been at Columbia.

Bohr Or Chicago. He had offers from both.

Margrethe He wouldn't leave Germany.

Bohr He wants to be there to rebuild German science when Hitler goes. He told Goudsmit.

Margrethe And if he's being watched it will all be reported upon. Who he sees. What he says to them. What they say to him.

Heisenberg I carry my surveillance around like an infectious disease. But then I happen to know that Bohr is also under surveillance.

Margrethe And you know you're being watched yourself.

Bohr By the Gestapo?

Heisenberg Docs he realise?

Bohr I've nothing to hide.

Margrethe By our fellow-Danes. It would be a terrible betrayal of all their trust in you if they thought you were collaborating.

Bohr Inviting an old friend to dinner is hardly collaborating.

Margrethe It might appear to be collaborating.

Bohr Yes. He's put us in a difficult position.

Margrethe I shall never forgive him.

Bohr He must have good reason. He must have very good reason.

Heisenberg This is going to be a deeply awkward occasion.

Margrethe   You won't talk about politics?

Bohr   We'll stick to physics. I assume it's physics he wants to talk to me about.

Margrethe   I think you must also assume that you and I aren't the only people who hear what's said in this house. If you want to speak privately you'd better go out in the open air.

Bohr   I shan't want to speak privately.

Margrethe   You could go for another of your walks together.

Heisenberg   Shall I be able to suggest a walk?

Bohr   I don't think we shall be going for any walks. Whatever he has to say he can say where everyone can hear it.

Margrethe   Some new idea he wants to try out on you, perhaps.

Bohr   What can it be, though? Where are we off to next?

Margrethe   So now of course your curiosity's aroused, in spite of everything.

Heisenberg   So now here I am, walking out through the autumn twilight to the Bohrs' house at Ny-Carlsberg. Followed, presumably, by my invisible shadow. What am I feeling? Fear, certainly – the touch of fear that one always feels for a teacher, for an employer, for a parent. Much worse fear about what I have to say. About how to express it. How to broach it in the first place. Worse fear still about what happens if I fail.

Margrethe   It's not something to do with the war?

Bohr   Heisenberg is a theoretical physicist. I don't think anyone has yet discovered a way you can use theoretical physics to kill people.

Margrethe   It couldn't be something about fission?

Bohr Fission? Why would he want to talk to me about fission?

Margrethe Because you're working on it.

Bohr Heisenberg isn't.

Margrethe Isn't he? Everybody else in the world seems to be. And you're the acknowledged authority.

Bohr He hasn't published on fission.

Margrethe It was Heisenberg who did all the original work on the physics of the nucleus. And he consulted you then, he consulted you at every step.

Bohr That was back in 1932. Fission's only been around for the last three years.

Margrethe But if the Germans were developing some kind of weapon based on nuclear fission . . .

Bohr My love, no one is going to develop a weapon based on nuclear fission.

Margrethe But if the Germans were trying to, Heisenberg would be involved.

Bohr There's no shortage of good German physicists.

Margrethe There's no shortage of good German physicists in America or Britain.

Bohr The Jews have gone, obviously.

Heisenberg Einstein, Wolfgang Pauli, Max Born . . . Otto Frisch, Lise Meitner. . . . We led the world in theoretical physics! Once.

Margrethe So who is there still working in Germany?

Bohr Sommerfeld, of course. Von Laue.

Margrethe Old men.

Bohr Wirtz. Harteck.

Margrethe Heisenberg is head and shoulders above all

of them.

Bohr   Otto Hahn – he's still there. He discovered fission, after all.

Margrethe   Hahn's a chemist. I thought that what Hahn discovered . . .

Bohr   . . . was that Enrico Fermi had discovered it in Rome four years earlier. Yes – he just didn't realise it was fission. It didn't occur to anyone that the uranium atom might have split, and turned into two atoms of barium. Not until Hahn and Strassmann did the analysis, and detected the barium.

Margrethe   Fermi's in Chicago.

Bohr   His wife's Jewish.

Margrethe   So Heisenberg would be in charge of the work?

Bohr   Margrethe, there is no work! John Wheeler and I did it all in 1939. One of the implications of our paper is that there's no way in the foreseeable future in which fission can be used to produce any kind of weapon.

Margrethe   Then why is everyone still working on it?

Bohr   Because there's an element of magic in it. You fire a neutron at the nucleus of a uranium atom and it splits into two atoms of barium. It's what the alchemists were trying to do – to turn one element into another.

Margrethe   So why is he coming?

Bohr   Now your curiosity's aroused.

Margrethe   My forebodings.

Heisenberg   I crunch over the familiar gravel to the Bohrs' front door, and tug at the familiar bell-pull. Fear, yes. And another sensation, that's become painfully familiar over the past year. A mixture of self-importance and sheer helpless absurdity – that of all the 2,000 million people in this world, I'm the one who's been charged with this impossible responsibility. . . . The heavy door swings open.

Bohr My dear Heisenberg!

Heisenberg My dear Bohr!

Bohr Come in, come in . . .

Margrethe And of course as soon as they catch sight of each other all their caution disappears. The old flames leap up from the ashes. If we can just negotiate all the treacherous little opening civilities . . .

Heisenberg I'm so touched you felt able to ask me.

Bohr We must try to go on behaving like human beings.

Heisenberg I realise how awkward it is.

Bohr We scarcely had a chance to do more than shake hands at lunch the other day.

Heisenberg And Margrethe I haven't seen . . .

Bohr Since you were here four years ago.

Margrethe Niels is right. You look older.

Heisenberg I had been hoping to see you both in 1938, at the congress in Warsaw . . .

Bohr I believe you had some personal trouble.

Heisenberg A little business in Berlin.

Margrethe In the Prinz-Albert-Strasse?

Heisenberg A slight misunderstanding.

Bohr We heard, yes. I'm so sorry.

Heisenberg These things happen. The question is now resolved. Happily resolved. Entirely resolved. . . . We should all have met in Zürich . . .

Bohr In September 1939.

Heisenberg And of course, sadly . . .

Bohr Sadly for us as well.

Margrethe A lot more sadly still for many people.

Heisenberg Yes. Indeed.

Bohr Well, there it is.

Heisenberg What can I say?

Margrethe What can any of us say, in the present circumstances?

Heisenberg No. And your sons?

Margrethe Are well, thank you. Elisabeth? The children?

Heisenberg Very well. They send their love, of course.

Margrethe They so much wanted to see each other, in spite of everything! But now the moment has come they're so busy avoiding each other's eye that they can scarcely see each other at all.

Heisenberg I wonder if you realise how much it means to me to be back here in Copenhagen. In this house. I have become rather isolated in these last few years.

Bohr I can imagine.

Margrethe Me he scarcely notices. I watch him discreetly from behind my expression of polite interest as he struggles on.

Heisenberg Have things here been difficult?

Bohr Difficult?

Margrethe Of course. He has to ask. He has to get it out of the way.

Bohr Difficult. . . . What can I say? We've not so far been treated to the gross abuses that have occurred elsewhere. The race laws have not been enforced.

Margrethe Yet.

Bohr A few months ago they started deporting Communists and other anti-German elements.

Heisenberg But you personally . . . ?

Bohr   Have been left strictly alone.

Heisenberg   I've been anxious about you.

Bohr   Kind of you. No call for sleepless nights in Leipzig so far, though.

Margrethe   Another silence. He's done his duty. Now he can begin to steer the conversation round to pleasanter subjects.

Heisenberg   Are you still sailing?

Bohr   Sailing?

Margrethe   Not a good start.

Bohr   No, no sailing.

Heisenberg   The Sound is . . . ?

Bohr   Mined.

Heisenberg   Of course.

Margrethe   I assume he won't ask if Niels has been ski-ing.

Heisenberg   You've managed to get some ski-ing?

Bohr   Ski-ing? In Denmark?

Heisenberg   In Norway. You used to go to Norway.

Bohr   I did, yes.

Heisenberg   But since Norway is also . . . well . . .

Bohr   Also occupied? Yes, that might make it easier. In fact I suppose we could now holiday almost anywhere in Europe.

Heisenberg   I'm sorry. I hadn't thought of it quite in those terms.

Bohr   Perhaps I'm being a little oversensitive.

Heisenberg   Of course not. I should have thought.

Margrethe   He must almost be starting to wish he was

back in the Prinz-Albert-Strasse.

Heisenberg   I don't suppose you feel you could ever come to Germany . . .

Margrethe   The boy's an idiot.

Bohr   My dear Heisenberg, it would be an easy mistake to make, to think that the citizens of a small nation, of a small nation overrun, wantonly and cruelly overrun, by its more powerful neighbour, don't have exactly the same feelings of national pride as their conquerors, exactly the same love of their country.

Margrethe   Niels, we agreed.

Bohr   To talk about physics, yes.

Margrethe   Not about politics.

Bohr   I'm sorry.

Heisenberg   No, no – I was simply going to say that I still have my old ski-hut at Bayrischzell. So if by any chance . . . at any time . . . for any reason . . .

Bohr   Most kind of you.

Heisenberg   Frau Schumacher in the bakery – you remember her?

Bohr   I remember Frau Schumacher.

Heisenberg   She still has the key.

Bohr   Perhaps Margrethe would be kind enough to sew a yellow star on my ski-jacket.

Heisenberg   Yes. Yes. Stupid of me.

Margrethe   Silence again. Those first brief sparks have disappeared, and the ashes have become very cold indeed. So now of course I'm starting to feel almost sorry for him. Sitting here all on his own in the midst of people who hate him, all on his own against the two of us. He looks younger again, like the boy who first came here in 1924. Younger than Christian would have been now. Shy and arrogant and anxious to be loved. Homesick and pleased to be away from home at last. And, yes, it's sad, because Niels loved him, he was a father to him.

Heisenberg So . . . what are you working on?

Margrethe And all he can do is press forward.

Bohr Fission, mostly.

Heisenberg I saw a couple of papers in the *Physical Review*. The velocity-range relations of fission fragments . . . ?

Bohr And something about the interactions of nuclei with deuterons. And you?

Heisenberg Various things.

Margrethe Fission?

Heisenberg I sometimes feel very envious of your cyclotron.

Margrethe Why? Are you working on fission yourself?

Heisenberg There are over thirty in the United States. Whereas in the whole of Germany . . . Well. . . . You still get to your country place, at any rate?

Bohr We still go to Tisvilde, yes.

Margrethe In the whole of Germany, you were going to say . . .

Bohr . . . there is not one single cyclotron.

Heisenberg So beautiful at this time of year. Tisvilde.

Bohr You haven't come to borrow the cyclotron, have you? That's not why you've come to Copenhagen?

Heisenberg That's not why I've come to Copenhagen.

Bohr I'm sorry. We mustn't jump to conclusions.

Heisenberg No, we must none of us jump to conclusions of any sort.

Margrethe We must wait patiently to be told.

Heisenberg   It's not always easy to explain things to the world at large.

Bohr   I realise that we must always be conscious of the wider audience our words may have. But the lack of cyclotrons in Germany is surely not a military secret.

Heisenberg   I've no idea what's a secret and what isn't.

Bohr   No secret, either, about why there aren't any. You can't say it but I can. It's because the Nazis have systematically undermined theoretical physics. Why? Because so many people working in the field were Jews. And why were so many of them Jews? Because theoretical physics, the sort of physics done by Einstein, by Schrödinger and Pauli, by Born and Sommerfeld, by you and me, was always regarded in Germany as inferior to experimental physics, and the theoretical chairs and lectureships were the only ones that Jews could get.

Margrethe   Physics, yes? Physics.

Bohr   This is physics.

Margrethe   It's also politics.

Heisenberg   The two are sometimes painfully difficult to keep apart.

Bohr   So, you saw those two papers. I haven't seen anything by you recently.

Heisenberg   No.

Bohr   Not like you. Too much teaching?

Heisenberg   I'm not teaching. Not at the moment.

Bohr   My dear Heisenberg – they haven't pushed you out of your chair at Leipzig? That's not what you've come to tell us?

Heisenberg   No, I'm still at Leipzig. For part of each week.

Bohr   And for the rest of the week?

Heisenberg Elsewhere. The problem is more work, not less.

Bohr I see. Do I?

Heisenberg Are you in touch with any of our friends in England? Born? Chadwick?

Bohr Heisenberg, we're under German occupation. Germany's at war with Britain.

Heisenberg I thought you might still have contacts of some sort. Or people in America? We're not at war with America.

Margrethe Yet.

Heisenberg You've heard nothing from Pauli, in Princeton? Goudsmit? Fermi?

Bohr What do you want to know?

Heisenberg I was simply curious ... I was thinking about Robert Oppenheimer the other day. I had a great set-to with him in Chicago in 1939.

Bohr About mesons.

Heisenberg Is he still working on mesons?

Bohr I'm quite out of touch.

Margrethe The only foreign visitor we've had was from Germany. Your friend Weizsäcker was here in March.

Heisenberg *My* friend? *Your* friend, too. I hope. You know he's come back to Copenhagen with me? He's very much hoping to see you again.

Margrethe When he came here in March he brought the head of the German Cultural Institute with him.

Heisenberg I'm sorry about that. He did it with the best of intentions. He may not have explained to you that the Institute is run by the Cultural Division of the Foreign Office. We have good friends in the foreign service. Particularly at the Embassy here.

Bohr   Of course. I knew his father when he was Ambassador in Copenhagen in the twenties.

Heisenberg   It hasn't changed so much since then, you know, the German foreign service.

Bohr   It's a department of the Nazi government.

Heisenberg   Germany is more complex than it may perhaps appear from the outside. The different organs of state have quite different traditions. Some departments remain stubbornly idiosyncratic, in spite of all attempts at reform. Particularly the foreign service. You know how attached diplomats are to outmoded conventions. Our people in the Embassy here are quite old-fashioned in the way they use their influence. They would certainly be trying to see that distinguished local citizens were able to work undisturbed.

Bohr   Are you telling me that I'm being protected by your friends in the Embassy?

Heisenberg   What I'm saying, in case Weizsäcker failed to make it clear, is that you would find congenial company there. I know people would be very honoured if you felt able to accept an occasional invitation.

Bohr   To cocktail parties at the Germany Embassy? To coffee and cakes with the Nazi plenipotentiary?

Heisenberg   To lectures, perhaps. To discussion groups. Social contacts of any sort could be helpful.

Bohr   I'm sure they could.

Heisenberg   Essential, perhaps, in certain circumstances.

Bohr   In what circumstances?

Heisenberg   I think we both know.

Bohr   Because I'm half-Jewish?

Heisenberg   We all at one time or another may need the help of our friends.

Bohr Is this why you've come to Copenhagen? To invite me to watch the deportation of my fellow-Danes from a grandstand seat in the windows of the German Embassy?

Heisenberg Bohr, please! Please! What else can I do? How else can I help? It's an impossibly difficult situation for you, I understand that. It's also an impossibly difficult one for me.

Bohr Yes. I'm sorry. I'm sure you also have the best of intentions.

Heisenberg Forget what I said. Unless ...

Bohr Unless I need to remember it.

Heisenberg In any case it's not why I've come.

Margrethe Perhaps you should simply say what it is you want to say.

Heisenberg What you and I often used to do in the old days was to take an evening stroll.

Bohr Often. Yes. In the old days.

Heisenberg You don't feel like a stroll this evening, for old times' sake?

Bohr A little chilly tonight, perhaps, for strolling.

Heisenberg This is so difficult. You remember where we first met?

Bohr Of course. At Göttingen in 1922.

Heisenberg At a lecture festival held in your honour.

Bohr It was a high honour. I was very conscious of it.

Heisenberg You were being honoured for two reasons. Firstly because you were a great physicist ...

Bohr Yes, yes.

Heisenberg ... and secondly because you were one of the very few people in Europe who were prepared to have dealings with Germany. The war had been over for four years, and we were still lepers. You held out your hand to us. You've always inspired love, you know that. Wherever you've been, wherever you've worked. Here in Denmark. In England, in America. But in Germany we worshipped you. Because you held out your hand to us.

Bohr　Germany's changed.

Heisenberg　Yes. Then we were down. And you could be generous.

Margrethe　And now you're up.

Heisenberg　And generosity's harder. But you held out your hand to us then, and we took it.

Bohr　Yes. . . . No! Not you. As a matter of fact. You bit it.

Heisenberg　Bit it?

Bohr　Bit my hand! You did! I held it out, in my most statesmanlike and reconciliatory way, and you gave it a very nasty nip.

Heisenberg　*I* did?

Bohr　The first time I ever set eyes on you. At one of those lectures I was giving in Göttingen.

Heisenberg　What are you talking about?

Bohr　You stood up and laid into me.

Heisenberg　Oh . . . I offered a few comments.

Bohr　Beautiful summer's day. The scent of roses drifting in from the gardens. Rows of eminent physicists and mathematicians, all nodding approval of my benevolence and wisdom. Suddenly, up jumps a cheeky young pup and tells me that my mathematics are wrong.

Heisenberg　They were wrong.

Bohr　How old were you?

Heisenberg　Twenty.

Bohr Two years younger than the century.

Heisenberg Not quite.

Bohr December 5th, yes?

Heisenberg 1.93 years younger than the century.

Bohr To be precise.

Heisenberg No – to two places of decimals. To be *precise*, 1.928 ... 7 ... 6 ... 7 ... 1 ...

Bohr I can always keep track of you, all the same. And the century.

Margrethe And Niels has suddenly decided to love him again, in spite of everything. Why? What happened? Was it the recollection of that summer's day in Göttingen? Or everything? Or nothing at all? Whatever it was, by the time we've sat down to dinner the cold ashes have started into flame once again.

Bohr You were always so combative! It was the same when we played table-tennis at Tisvilde. You looked as if you were trying to kill me.

Heisenberg I wanted to win. Of course I wanted to win. *You* wanted to win.

Bohr I wanted an agreeable game of table-tennis.

Heisenberg You couldn't see the expression on your face.

Bohr I could see the expression on yours.

Heisenberg What about those games of poker in the ski-hut at Bayrischzell, then? You once cleaned us all out! You remember that? With a non-existent straight! We're all mathematicians – we're all counting the cards – we're 90 per cent certain he hasn't got anything. But on he goes, raising us, raising us. This insane confidence. Until our faith in mathematical probability begins to waver, and one by one we all throw in.

Bohr I thought I *had* a straight! I misread the cards! I bluffed myself!

Margrethe Poor Niels.

Heisenberg Poor Niels? He won! He bankrupted us! You were insanely competitive! He got us all playing poker once with imaginary cards!

Bohr You played chess with Weizsäcker on an imaginary board!

Margrethe Who won?

Bohr Need you ask? At Bayrischzell we'd ski down from the hut to get provisions, and he'd make even that into some kind of race! You remember? When we were there with Weizsäcker and someone? You got out a stop-watch.

Heisenberg It took poor Weizsäcker eighteen minutes.

Bohr You were down there in ten, of course.

Heisenberg Eight.

Bohr I don't recall how long I took.

Heisenberg Forty-five minutes.

Bohr Thank you.

Margrethe Some rather swift ski-ing going on here, I think.

Heisenberg Your ski-ing was like your science. What were you waiting for? Me and Weizsäcker to come back and suggest some slight change of emphasis?

Bohr Probably.

Heisenberg You were doing seventeen drafts of each slalom?

Margrethe And without me there to type them out.

Bohr At least I knew where I was. At the speed you were going you were up against the uncertainty relationship. If you knew where you were when you were down you didn't know how fast you'd got there. If you knew how fast you'd been going you didn't know you were down.

Heisenberg I certainly didn't stop to think about it.

Bohr Not to criticise, but that's what might be criticised with some of your science.

Heisenberg I usually got there, all the same.

Bohr You never cared what got destroyed on the way, though. As long as the mathematics worked out you were satisfied.

Heisenberg If something works it works.

Bohr But the question is always, What does the mathematics mean, in plain language? What are the philosophical implications?

Heisenberg I always knew you'd be picking your way step by step down the slope behind me, digging all the capsized meanings and implications out of the snow.

Margrethe The faster you ski the sooner you're across the cracks and crevasses.

Heisenberg The faster you ski the better you think.

Bohr Not to disagree, but that is most ... most interesting.

Heisenberg By which you mean it's nonsense. But it's not nonsense. Decisions make themselves when you're coming downhill at seventy kilometres an hour. Suddenly there's the edge of nothingness in front of you. Swerve left? Swerve right? Or think about it and die? In your head you swerve both ways ...

Margrethe Like that particle.

Heisenberg What particle?

Margrethe The one that you said goes through two different slits at the same time.

Heisenberg Oh, in our old thought-experiment. Yes. Yes!

Margrethe Or Schrödinger's wretched cat.

Heisenberg That's alive and dead at the same time.

Margrethe Poor beast.

Bohr My love, it was an imaginary cat.

Margrethe I know.

Bohr Locked away with an imaginary phial of cyanide.

Margrethe I know, I know.

Heisenberg So the particle's here, the particle's there . . .

Bohr The cat's alive, the cat's dead . . .

Margrethe You've swerved left, you've swerved right . . .

Heisenberg Until the experiment is over, this is the point, until the sealed chamber is opened, the abyss detoured; and it turns out that the particle has met itself again, the cat's dead . . .

Margrethe And you're alive.

Bohr Not so fast, Heisenberg . . .

Heisenberg The swerve itself was the decision.

Bohr Not so fast, not so fast!

Heisenberg Isn't that how you shot Hendrik Casimir dead?

Bohr Hendrik Casimir?

Heisenberg When he was working here at the Institute.

Bohr I never shot Hendrik Casimir.

Heisenberg You told me you did.

Bohr It was George Gamow. I shot George Gamow. *You* don't know – it was long after your time.

Heisenberg Bohr, you shot Hendrik Casimir.

Bohr Gamow, Gamow. Because he insisted that it was always quicker to act than to react. To make a decision to do something rather than respond to someone else's doing it.

Heisenberg And for that you shot him?

Bohr It was him! He went out and bought a pair of pistols! He puts one in his pocket, I put one in mine, and we get on with the day's work. Hours go by, and we're arguing ferociously about – I can't remember – our problems with the nitrogen nucleus, I expect – when suddenly Gamow reaches into his pocket . . .

Heisenberg Cap-pistols.

Bohr Cap-pistols, yes. Of course.

Heisenberg Margrethe was looking a little worried.

Margrethe No – a little surprised. At the turn of events.

Bohr Now you remember how quick he was.

Heisenberg Casimir?

Bohr Gamow.

Heisenberg Not as quick as me.

Bohr Of course not. But compared with me.

Heisenberg A fast neutron. However, or so you're going to tell me . . .

Bohr However, yes, before his gun is even out of his pocket . . .

Heisenberg You've drafted your reply.

Margrethe I've typed it out.

Heisenberg You've checked it with Klein.

Margrethe I've retyped it.

Heisenberg You've submitted it to Pauli in Hamburg.

Margrethe   I've retyped it again.

Bohr   Before his gun is even out of his pocket, mine is in my hand.

Heisenberg   And poor Casimir has been blasted out of existence.

Bohr   Except that it was Gamow.

Heisenberg   It was Casimir! He told me!

Bohr   Yes, well, one of the two.

Heisenberg   Both of them simultaneously alive and dead in our memories.

Bohr   Like a pair of Schrödinger cats. Where were we?

Heisenberg   Ski-ing. Or music. That's another thing that decides everything for you. I play the piano and the way seems to open in front of me – all I have to do is follow. That's how I had my one success with women. At a musical evening at the Bückings in Leipzig – we've assembled a piano trio. 1937, just when all my troubles with the . . . when my troubles are coming to a head. We're playing the Beethoven G major. We finish the scherzo, and I look up from the piano to see if the others are ready to start the final presto. And in that instant I catch a glimpse of a young woman sitting at the side of the room. Just the briefest glimpse, but of course at once I've carried her off to Bayrischzell, we're engaged, we're married, etc – the usual hopeless romantic fantasies. Then off we go into the presto, and it's terrifyingly fast – so fast there's no time to be afraid. And suddenly everything in the world seems easy. We reach the end and I just carry on ski-ing. Get myself introduced to the young woman – see her home – and, yes, a week later I've carried her off to Bayrischzell – another week and we're engaged – three months and we're married. All on the sheer momentum of that presto!

Bohr   You were saying you felt isolated. But you do have a companion, after all.

Heisenberg   Music?

Bohr   Elisabeth!

Heisenberg   Oh. Yes. Though, what with the children, and so on ... I've always envied the way you and Margrethe manage to talk about everything. Your work. Your problems. Me, no doubt.

Bohr   I was formed by nature to be a mathematically curious entity: not one but half of two.

Heisenberg   Mathematics becomes very odd when you apply it to people. One plus one can add up to so many different sums ...

Margrethe   Silence. What's he thinking about now? His life? Or ours?

Bohr   So many things we think about at the same time. Our lives and our physics.

Margrethe   All the things that come into our heads out of nowhere.

Bohr   Our private consolations. Our private agonies.

Heisenberg   Silence. And of course they're thinking about their children again.

Margrethe   The same bright things. The same dark things. Back and back they come.

Heisenberg   Their four children living, and their two children dead.

Margrethe   Harald. Lying alone in that ward.

Bohr   She's thinking about Christian and Harald.

Heisenberg   The two lost boys. Harald ...

Bohr   All those years alone in that terrible ward.

Heisenberg   And Christian. The firstborn. The eldest son.

Bohr   And once again I see those same few moments that

I see every day.

Heisenberg Those short moments on the boat, when the tiller slams over in the heavy sea, and Christian is falling.

Bohr If I hadn't let him take the helm . . .

Heisenberg Those long moments in the water.

Bohr Those endless moments in the water.

Heisenberg When he's struggling towards the lifebuoy.

Bohr So near to touching it.

Margrethe I'm at Tisvilde. I look up from my work. There's Niels in the doorway, silently watching me. He turns his head away, and I know at once what's happened.

Bohr So near, so near! So slight a thing!

Heisenberg Again and again the tiller slams over. Again and again . . .

Margrethe Niels turns his head away . . .

Bohr Christian reaches for the lifebuoy . . .

Heisenberg But about some things even they never speak.

Bohr About some things even we only think.

Margrethe Because there's nothing to be said.

Bohr Well . . . perhaps we *should* be warm enough. You suggested a stroll.

Heisenberg In fact the weather is remarkably warm.

Bohr We shan't be long.

Heisenberg A week at most.

Bohr What – our great hike through Zealand?

Heisenberg We went to Elsinore. I often think about what you said there.

Bohr You don't mind, my love? Half-an-hour?

Heisenberg   An hour, perhaps. No, the whole
appearance of Elsinore, you said, was changed by our
knowing that Hamlet had lived there. Every dark corner
there reminds us of the darkness inside the human soul . . .

Margrethe   So, they're walking again. He's done it. And
if they're walking they're talking. Talking in a rather
different way, no doubt – I've typed out so much in my
time about how differently particles behave when they're
unobserved . . . I knew Niels would never hold out if they
could just get through the first few minutes. If only out of
curiosity. . . . Now they're started an hour will mean two, of
course, perhaps three. . . . The first thing they ever did was
to go for a walk together. At Göttingen, after that lecture.
Niels immediately went to look for the presumptuous young
man who'd queried his mathematics, and swept him off for
a tramp in the country. Walk – talk – make his
acquaintance. And when Heisenberg arrived here to work
for him, off they go again, on their great tour of Zealand.
A lot of this century's physics they did in the open air.
Strolling around the forest paths at Tisvilde. Going down to
the beach with the children. Heisenberg holding Christian's
hand. They talked on the boat a lot. Was Christian ever on
the boat with them? No, he was too young for sailing
then. . . . Yes, and every evening in Copenhagen, after
dinner, they'd walk round Faelled Park behind the Institute,
or out along Langelinie into the harbour. Walk, and talk.
Long, long before walls had ears . . . But this time, in 1941,
their walk takes a different course. Ten minutes after they
set out . . . they're back! I've scarcely had the table cleared
when there's Niels in the doorway. I see at once how upset
he is – he can't look me in the eye.

Bohr   Heisenberg wants to say goodbye. He's leaving.

Margrethe   *He* won't look at me, either.

Heisenberg   Thank you. A delightful evening. Almost
like old times. So kind of you.

Margrethe   You'll have some coffee? A glass of
something?

Heisenberg   I have to get back and prepare for my lecture.

Margrethe   But you'll come and see us again before you leave?

Bohr   He has a great deal to do.

Margrethe   It's like the worst moments of 1927 all over again, when Niels came back from Norway and first read Heisenberg's uncertainty paper. Something they both seemed to have forgotten about earlier in the evening, though I hadn't. Perhaps they've both suddenly remembered that time. Only from the look on their faces something even worse has happened.

Heisenberg   Forgive me if I've done or said anything that . . .

Bohr   Yes, yes.

Heisenberg   It meant a great deal to me, being here with you both again. More perhaps than you realise.

Margrethe   It was a pleasure for us. Our love to Elisabeth.

Bohr   Of course.

Margrethe   And the children.

Heisenberg   Perhaps, when this war is over. . . . If we're all spared. . . . Goodbye.

Margrethe   Politics?

Bohr   Physics. He's not right, though. How can he be right? John Wheeler and I . . .

Margrethe   A breath of air as we talk, why not?

Bohr   A breath of air?

Margrethe   A turn around the garden. Healthier than staying indoors, perhaps.

Bohr   Oh. Yes.

Margrethe   For everyone concerned.

Bohr   Yes. Thank you. . . . How can he possibly be right? Wheeler and I went through the whole thing in 1939.

Margrethe   What did he say?

Bohr   Nothing. I don't know. I was too angry to take it in.

Margrethe   Something about fission?

Bohr   What happens in fission? You fire a neutron at a uranium nucleus, it splits, and it releases energy.

Margrethe   A huge amount of energy. Yes?

Bohr   About enough to move a speck of dust. But it also releases two or three more neutrons. Each of which has the chance of splitting another nucleus.

Margrethe   So then those two or three split nuclei each release energy in their turn?

Bohr   And two or three more neutrons.

Heisenberg   You start a trickle of snow sliding as you ski. The trickle becomes a snowball . . .

Bohr   An ever-widening chain of split nuclei forks through the uranium, doubling and quadrupling in millionths of a second from one generation to the next. First two splits, let's say for simplicity. Then two squared, two cubed, two to the fourth, two to the fifth, two to the sixth . . .

Heisenberg   The thunder of the gathering avalanche echoes from all the surrounding mountains . . .

Bohr   Until eventually, after, let's say, eighty generations, 2^{80} specks of dust have been moved. 2^{80} is a number with 24 noughts. Enough specks of dust to constitute a city, and all who live in it.

Heisenberg   But there is a catch.

Bohr   There is a catch, thank God. Natural uranium consists of two different isotopes, U-238 and U-235. Less than one per cent of it is U-235, and this tiny fraction is the only part of it that's fissionable by fast neutrons.

Heisenberg This was Bohr's great insight. Another of his amazing intuitions. It came to him when he was at Princeton in 1939, walking across the campus with Wheeler. A characteristic Bohr moment – I wish I'd been there to enjoy it. Five minutes deep silence as they walked, then: 'Now hear this – I have understood everything.'

Bohr In fact it's a double catch. 238 is not only impossible to fission by fast neutrons – it also absorbs them. So, very soon after the chain reaction starts, there aren't enough fast neutrons left to fission the 235.

Heisenberg And the chain stops.

Bohr Now, you can fission the 235 with slow neutrons as well. But then the chain reaction occurs more slowly than the uranium blows itself apart.

Heisenberg So again the chain stops.

Bohr What all this means is that an explosive chain reaction will never occur in natural uranium. To make an explosion you will have to separate out pure 235. And to make the chain long enough for a large explosion . . .

Heisenberg Eighty generations, let's say . . .

Bohr . . . you would need many tons of it. And it's extremely difficult to separate.

Heisenberg Tantalisingly difficult.

Bohr Mercifully difficult. The best estimates, when I was in America in 1939, were that to produce even one gram of U-235 would take 26,000 years. By which time, surely, this war will be over. So he's wrong, you see, he's wrong! Or could *I* be wrong? Could I have miscalculated? Let me see. . . . What are the absorption rates for fast neutrons in 238? What's the mean free path of slow neutrons in 235 . . . ?

Margrethe But what exactly had Heisenberg said? That's what everyone wanted to know, then and forever after.

Bohr It's what the British wanted to know, as soon as Chadwick managed to get in touch with me. What exactly did Heisenberg say?

Heisenberg And what exactly did Bohr reply? That was of course the first thing my colleagues asked me when I got back to Germany.

Margrethe What did Heisenberg tell Niels – what did Niels reply? The person who wanted to know most of all was Heisenberg himself.

Bohr You mean when he came back to Copenhagen after the war, in 1947?

Margrethe Escorted this time not by unseen agents of the Gestapo, but by a very conspicuous minder from British intelligence.

Bohr I think he wanted various things.

Margrethe Two things. Food-parcels . . .

Bohr For his family in Germany. They were on the verge of starvation.

Margrethe And for you to agree what you'd said to each other in 1941.

Bohr The conversation went wrong almost as fast as it did before.

Margrethe You couldn't even agree where you'd walked that night.

Heisenberg Where we walked? Faelled Park, of course. Where we went so often in the old days.

Margrethe But Faelled Park is behind the Institute, eight or nine kilometres away from where we live!

Heisenberg I can see the drift of autumn leaves under the street-lamps next to the bandstand.

Bohr Yes, because you remember it as October!

Margrethe And it was September.

Bohr No fallen leaves!

Margrethe And it was 1941. No street-lamps!

Bohr I thought we hadn't got any further than my study. What I can see is the drift of papers under the reading-lamp on my desk.

Heisenberg We must have been outside! What I was going to say was treasonable. If I'd been overheard I'd have been executed.

Margrethe So what was this mysterious thing you said?

Heisenberg There's no mystery about it. There never was any mystery. I remember it absolutely clearly, because my life was at stake, and I chose my words very carefully. I simply asked you if as a physicist one had the moral right to work on the practical exploitation of atomic energy. Yes?

Bohr I don't recall.

Heisenberg You don't recall, no, because you immediately became alarmed. You stopped dead in your tracks.

Bohr I was horrified.

Heisenberg Horrified. Good, you remember that. You stood there gazing at me, horrified.

Bohr Because the implication was obvious. That you *were* working on it.

Heisenberg And you jumped to the conclusion that I was trying to provide Hitler with nuclear weapons.

Bohr And you were!

Heisenberg No! A reactor! That's what we were trying to build! A machine to produce power! To generate electricity, to drive ships!

Bohr You didn't say anything about a reactor.

Heisenberg I didn't say anything about anything! Not in so many words. I couldn't! I'd no idea how much could be overheard. How much you'd repeat to others.

Bohr   But then I asked you if you actually thought that uranium fission could be used for the construction of weapons.

Heisenberg   Ah! It's coming back!

Bohr   And I clearly remember what you replied.

Heisenberg   I said I now knew that it could be.

Bohr   This is what really horrified me.

Heisenberg   Because you'd always been confident that weapons would need 235, and that we could never separate enough of it.

Bohr   A reactor – yes, maybe, because there it's not going to blow itself apart. You can keep the chain reaction going with slow neutrons in natural uranium.

Heisenberg   What we'd realised, though, was that if we could once get the reactor going . . .

Bohr   The 238 in the natural uranium would absorb the fast neutrons . . .

Heisenberg   Exactly as you predicted in 1939 – everything we were doing was based on that fundamental insight of yours. The 238 would absorb the fast neutrons. And would be transformed by them into a new element altogether.

Bohr   Neptunium. Which would decay in its turn into another new element . . .

Heisenberg   At least as fissile as the 235 that we couldn't separate . . .

Margrethe   Plutonium.

Heisenberg   Plutonium.

Bohr   I should have worked it out for myself.

Heisenberg   If we could build a reactor we could build

bombs. That's what had brought me to Copenhagen. But none of this could I say. And at this point you stopped listening. The bomb had already gone off inside your head. I realised we were heading back towards the house. Our walk was over. Our one chance to talk had gone forever.

Bohr   Because I'd grasped the central point already. That one way or another you saw the possibility of supplying Hitler with nuclear weapons.

Heisenberg   You grasped at least four different central points, all of them wrong. You told Rozental that I'd tried to pick your brains about fission. You told Weisskopf that I'd asked you what you knew about the Allied nuclear programme. Chadwick thought I was hoping to persuade you that there was no German programme. But then you seem to have told some people that I'd tried to recruit you to work on it!

Bohr   Very well. Let's start all over again from the beginning. No Gestapo in the shadows this time. No British intelligence officer. No one watching us at all.

Margrethe   Only me.

Bohr   Only Margrethe. We're going to make the whole thing clear to Margrethe. You know how strongly I believe that we don't do science for ourselves, that we do it so we can explain to others . . .

Heisenberg   In plain language.

Bohr   In plain language. Not your view, I know – you'd be happy to describe what you were up to purely in differential equations if you could – but for Margrethe's sake . . .

Heisenberg   Plain language.

Bohr   Plain language. All right, so here we are, walking along the street once more. And this time I'm absolutely calm, I'm listening intently. What is it you want to say?

Heisenberg   It's not just what *I* want to say! The whole

German nuclear team in Berlin! Not Diebner, of course, not the Nazis – but Weizsäcker, Hahn, Wirtz, Jensen, Houtermanns – they all wanted me to come and discuss it with you. We all see you as a kind of spiritual father.

Margrethe The Pope. That's what you used to call Niels behind his back. And now you want him to give you absolution.

Heisenberg Absolution? No!

Margrethe According to your colleague Jensen.

Heisenberg Absolution is the last thing I want!

Margrethe You told one historian that Jensen had expressed it perfectly.

Heisenberg Did I? Absolution. . . . Is that what I've come for? It's like trying to remember who was at that lunch you gave me at the Institute. Around the table sit all the different explanations for everything I did. I turn to look . . . Petersen, Rozental, and . . . yes . . . now the word absolution is taking its place among them all . . .

Margrethe Though I thought absolution was granted for sins past and repented, not for sins intended and yet to be committed.

Heisenberg Exactly! That's why I was so shocked!

Bohr *You* were shocked?

Heisenberg Because you *did* give me absolution! That's exactly what you did! As we were hurrying back to the house. You muttered something about everyone in wartime being obliged to do his best for his own country. Yes?

Bohr Heaven knows what I said. But now here I am, profoundly calm and conscious, weighing my words. You don't want absolution. I understand. You want me to tell you *not* to do it? All right. I put my hand on your arm. I look you in the eye in my most papal way. Go back to Germany, Heisenberg. Gather your colleagues together in the laboratory. The whole team – Weizsäcker, Hahn,

Wirtz, Jensen, Houtermanns, all the assistants and
technicians. Get up on a table and tell them: 'Niels Bohr
says that in his considered judgment supplying a homicidal
maniac with an improved instrument of mass murder is . . .'
What shall I say? '. . . an interesting idea.' No, not even an
interesting idea. '. . . a really rather seriously uninteresting
idea.' What happens? You all fling down your Geiger
counters?

Heisenberg   Obviously not.

Bohr   Because they'll arrest you.

Heisenberg   Whether they arrest us or not it won't make
any difference. In fact it will make things worse. I'm
running my programme for the Kaiser Wilhelm Institute.
But there's a rival one at Army Ordnance, run by Kurt
Diebner, and he's a party member. If I go they'll simply
get Diebner to take over my programme as well. He should
be running it anyway. Wirtz and the rest of them only
smuggled me in to keep Diebner and the Nazis out of it.
My one hope is to remain in control.

Bohr   So you don't want me to say yes and you don't
want me to say no.

Heisenberg   What I want is for you to listen carefully to
what I'm going on to say next, instead of running off down
the street like a madman.

Bohr   Very well. Here I am, walking very slowly and
popishly. And I listen most carefully as you tell me . . .

Heisenberg   That nuclear weapons will require an
enormous technical effort.

Bohr   True.

Heisenberg   That they will suck up huge resources.

Bohr   Huge resources. Certainly.

Heisenberg   That sooner or later governments will have
to turn to scientists and ask whether it's worth committing
those resources – whether there's any hope of producing

the weapons in time for them to be used.

Bohr   Of course, but . . .

Heisenberg   Wait. So they will have to come to you and me. We are the ones who will have to advise them whether to go ahead or not. In the end the decision will be in our hands, whether we like it or not.

Bohr   And that's what you want to tell me?

Heisenberg   That's what I want to tell you.

Bohr   That's why you have come all this way, with so much difficulty? That's why you have thrown away nearly twenty years of friendship? Simply to tell me that?

Heisenberg   Simply to tell you that.

Bohr   But, Heisenberg, this is more mysterious than ever! What are you telling it me *for*? What am I supposed to do about it? The government of occupied Denmark isn't going to come to me and ask me whether we should produce nuclear weapons!

Heisenberg   No, but sooner or later, if I manage to remain in control of our programme, the German government is going to come to *me*! They will ask *me* whether to continue or not! *I* will have to decide what to tell them!

Bohr   Then you have an easy way out of your difficulties. You tell them the simple truth that you've just told me. You tell them how difficult it will be. And perhaps they'll be discouraged. Perhaps they'll lose interest.

Heisenberg   But, Bohr, where will that lead? What will be the consequences if we manage to fail?

Bohr   What can I possibly tell you that you can't tell yourself?

Heisenberg   There was a report in a Stockholm paper that the Americans are working on an atomic bomb.

Bohr   Ah. Now it comes, now it comes. Now I

understand everything. You think I have contacts with the Americans?

Heisenberg You may. It's just conceivable. If anyone in Occupied Europe does it will be you.

Bohr So you *do* want to know about the Allied nuclear programme.

Heisenberg I simply want to know if there is one. Some hint. Some clue. I've just betrayed my country and risked my life to warn you of the German programme . . .

Bohr And now I'm to return the compliment?

Heisenberg Bohr, I have to know! I'm the one who has to decide! If the Allies are building a bomb, what am I choosing for my country? You said it would be easy to imagine that one might have less love for one's country if it's small and defenceless. Yes, and it would be another easy mistake to make, to think that one loved one's country less because it happened to be in the wrong. Germany is where I was born. Germany is where I became what I am. Germany is all the faces of my childhood, all the hands that picked me up when I fell, all the voices that encouraged me and set me on my way, all the hearts that speak to my heart. Germany is my widowed mother and my impossible brother. Germany is my wife. Germany is our children. I have to know what I'm deciding for them! Is it another defeat? Another nightmare like the nightmare I grew up with? Bohr, my childhood in Munich came to an end in anarchy and civil war. Are more children going to starve, as we did? Are they going to have to spend winter nights as I did when I was a schoolboy, crawling on my hands and knees through the enemy lines, creeping out into the country under cover of darkness in the snow to find food for my family? Are they going to sit up all night, as I did at the age of seventeen, guarding some terrified prisoner, talking to him and talking to him through the small hours, because he's going to be executed in the morning?

Bohr But, my dear Heisenberg, there's nothing I can tell you. I've no idea whether there's an Allied nuclear programme.

Heisenberg It's just getting under way even as you and I are talking. And maybe I'm choosing something worse even than defeat. Because the bomb they're building is to be used on us. On the evening of Hiroshima Oppenheimer said it was his one regret. That they hadn't produced the bomb in time to use on Germany.

Bohr He tormented himself afterwards.

Heisenberg Afterwards, yes. At least we tormented ourselves a little beforehand. Did a single one of them stop to think, even for one brief moment, about what they were doing? Did Oppenheimer? Did Fermi, or Teller, or Szilard? Did Einstein, when he wrote to Roosevelt in 1939 and urged him to finance research on the bomb? Did you, when you escaped from Copenhagen two years later, and went to Los Alamos?

Bohr My dear, good Heisenberg, we weren't supplying the bomb to Hitler!

Heisenberg You weren't dropping it on Hitler, either. You were dropping it on anyone who was in reach. On old men and women in the street, on mothers and their children. And if you'd produced it in time they would have been my fellow-countrymen. My wife. My children. That was the intention. Yes?

Bohr That was the intention.

Heisenberg You never had the slightest conception of what happens when bombs are dropped on cities. Even conventional bombs. None of you ever experienced it. Not a single one of you. I walked back from the centre of Berlin to the suburbs one night, after one of the big raids. No transport moving, of course. The whole city on fire. Even the puddles in the streets are burning. They're puddles of molten phosphorus. It gets on your shoes like some kind of incandescent dog-muck – I have to keep scraping it off – as if the streets have been fouled by the hounds of hell. It would have made you laugh – my shoes keep bursting into flame. All around me, I suppose, there are people trapped, people in various stages of burning to death. And all I can think is, How will I ever get hold of another pair of shoes in times like these?

Bohr   You know why Allied scientists worked on the bomb.

Heisenberg   Of course. Fear.

Bohr   The same fear that was consuming you. Because they were afraid that *you* were working on it.

Heisenberg   But, Bohr, you could have told them!

Bohr   Told them what?

Heisenberg   What I told you in 1941! That the choice is in our hands! In mine – in Oppenheimer's! That if I can tell them the simple truth when they ask me, the simple discouraging truth, so can he!

Bohr   This is what you want from me? Not to tell you what the Americans are doing but to stop them?

Heisenberg   To tell them that we can stop it together.

Bohr   I had no contact with the Americans!

Heisenberg   You did with the British.

Bohr   Only later.

Heisenberg   The Gestapo intercepted the message you sent them about our meeting.

Margrethe   And passed it to you?

Heisenberg   Why not? They'd begun to trust me. This is what gave me the possibility of remaining in control of events.

Bohr   Not to criticise, Heisenberg, but if this is your plan in coming to Copenhagen, it's . . . what can I say? It's most interesting.

Heisenberg It's not a plan. It's a hope. Not even a hope. A microscopically fine thread of possibility. A wild improbability. Worth trying, though, Bohr! Worth trying, surely! But already you're too angry to understand what I'm saying.

Margrethe No – why he's angry is because he *is* beginning to understand! The Germans drive out most of their best physicists because they're Jews. America and Britain give them sanctuary. Now it turns out that this might offer the Allies a hope of salvation. And at once you come howling to Niels begging him to persuade them to give it up.

Bohr Margrethe, my love, perhaps we should try to express ourselves a little more temperately.

Margrethe But the gall of it! The sheer, breathtaking gall of it!

Bohr Bold ski-ing, I have to say.

Heisenberg But, Bohr, we're not ski-ing now! We're not playing table-tennis! We're not juggling with cap-pistols and non-existent cards! I refused to believe it, when I first heard the news of Hiroshima. I thought that it was just one of the strange dreams we were living in at the time. They'd got stranger and stranger, God knows, as Germany fell into ruins in those last months of the war. But by then we were living in the strangest of them all. The ruins had suddenly vanished – just the way things do in dreams – and all at once we're in a stately home in the middle of the English countryside. We've been rounded up by the British – the whole team, everyone who worked on atomic research – and we've been spirited away. To Farm Hall, in Huntingdonshire, in the water-meadows of the River Ouse. Our families in Germany are starving, and there are we sitting down each evening to an excellent formal dinner with our charming host, the British officer in charge of us. It's like a pre-war house-party – one of those house-parties in a play, that's cut off from any contact with the outside world, where you know the guests have all been invited for

some secret sinister purpose. No one knows we're there —
no one in England, no one in Germany, not even our
families. But the war's over. What's happening? Perhaps, as
in a play, we're going to be quietly murdered, one by one.
In the meanwhile it's all delightfully civilised. I entertain the
party with Beethoven piano sonatas. Major Rittner, our
hospitable gaoler, reads Dickens to us, to improve our
English. . . . Did these things really happen to me . . . ? We
wait for the point of it all to be revealed to us. Then one
evening it is. And it's even more grotesque than the one we
were fearing. It's on the radio: you have actually done the
deed that we were tormenting ourselves about. That's why
we're there, dining with our gracious host, listening to our
Dickens. We've been kept locked up to stop us discussing
the subject with anyone until it's too late. When Major
Rittner tells us I simply refuse to believe it until I hear it
with my own ears on the nine o'clock news. We'd no idea
how far ahead you'd got. I can't describe the effect it has
on us. You play happily with your toy cap-pistol. Then
someone else picks it up and pulls the trigger . . . and all at
once there's blood everywhere and people screaming,
because it wasn't a toy at all. . . . We sit up half the night,
talking about it, trying to take it in. We're all literally in
shock.

Margrethe   Because it had been done? Or because it
wasn't you who'd done it?

Heisenberg   Both. Both. Otto Hahn wants to kill himself,
because it was he who discovered fission, and he can see
the blood on his hands. Gerlach, our old Nazi co-ordinator,
also wants to die, because his hands are so shamefully
clean. You've done it, though. You've built the bomb.

Bohr   Yes.

Heisenberg   And you've used it on a living target.

Bohr   On a living target.

Margrethe   You're not suggesting that Niels did anything
wrong in working at Los Alamos?

Heisenberg Of course not. Bohr has never done anything wrong.

Margrethe The decision had been taken long before Niels arrived. The bomb would have been built whether Niels had gone or not.

Bohr In any case, my part was very small.

Heisenberg Oppenheimer described you as the team's father-confessor.

Bohr It seems to be my role in life.

Heisenberg He said you made a great contribution.

Bohr Spiritual, possibly. Not practical.

Heisenberg Fermi says it was you who worked out how to trigger the Nagasaki bomb.

Bohr I put forward an idea.

Margrethe You're not implying that there's anything that *Niels* needs to explain or defend?

Heisenberg No one has ever expected him to explain or defend anything. He's a profoundly good man.

Bohr It's not a question of goodness. I was spared the decision.

Heisenberg Yes, and I was not. So explaining and defending myself was how I spent the last thirty years of my life. When I went to America in 1949 a lot of physicists wouldn't even shake my hand. Hands that had actually built the bomb wouldn't touch mine.

Margrethe And let me tell you, if you think you're making it any clearer to me now, you're not.

Bohr Margrethe, I understand his feelings . . .

Margrethe I don't. I'm as angry as you were before! It's so easy to make you feel conscience-stricken. Why should he transfer his burden to you? Because what does he do after his great consultation with you? He goes back to

Berlin and tells the Nazis that hc can produce atomic bombs!

Heisenberg   But what I stress is the difficulty of separating 235.

Margrethe   You tell them about plutonium.

Heisenberg   I tell some of the minor officials. I have to keep people's hopes alive!

Margrethe   Otherwise they'll send for the other one.

Heisenberg   Diebner. Very possibly.

Margrethe   There's always a Diebner at hand ready to take over our crimes.

Heisenberg   Diebner might manage to get a little further than me.

Bohr   Diebner?

Heisenberg   Might. Just possibly might.

Bohr   He hasn't a quarter of your ability!

Heisenberg   Not a tenth of it. But he has ten times the eagerness to do it. It might be a very different story if it's Diebner who puts the case at our meeting with Albert Speer, instead of me.

Margrethe   The famous meeting with Speer.

Heisenberg   But this is when it counts. This is the real moment of decision. It's June 1942. Nine months after my trip to Copenhagen. All research cancelled by Hitler unless it produces immediate results – and Speer is the sole arbiter of what will qualify. Now, we've just got the first sign that our reactor's going to work. Our first increase in neutrons. Not much – thirteen per cent – but it's a start.

Bohr   June 1942? You're slightly ahead of Fermi in Chicago.

Heisenberg   Only we don't know that. But the RAF have begun terror-bombing. They've obliterated half of Lübeck, and the whole centre of Rostock and Cologne.

We're desperate for new weapons to strike back with. If ever there's a moment to make our case, this is it.

Margrethe You don't ask him for the funding to continue?

Heisenberg To continue with the reactor? Of course I do. But I ask for so little that he doesn't take the programme seriously.

Margrethe Do you tell him the reactor will produce plutonium?

Heisenberg I don't tell him the reactor will produce plutonium. Not Speer, no. I don't tell him the reactor will produce plutonium.

Bohr A striking omission, I have to admit.

Heisenberg And what happens? It works! He gives us barely enough money to keep the reactor programme ticking over. And that is the end of the German atomic bomb. That is the end of it.

Margrethe You go on with the reactor, though.

Heisenberg We go on with the reactor. Of course. Because now there's no risk of getting it running in time to produce enough plutonium for a bomb. No, we go on with the reactor all right. We work like madmen on the reactor. We have to drag it all the way across Germany, from east to west, from Berlin to Swabia, to get it away from the bombing, to keep it out of the hands of the Russians. Diebner tries to hijack it on the way. We get it away from him, and we set it up in a little village in the Swabian Jura.

Bohr This is Haigerloch?

Heisenberg There's a natural shelter there – the village inn has a wine-cellar cut into the base of a cliff. We dig a hole in the floor for the reactor, and I keep that programme going, I keep it under my control, until the bitter end.

Bohr   But, Heisenberg, with respect now, with the greatest respect, you couldn't even keep the reactor under your control. That reactor was going to kill you.

Heisenberg   It wasn't put to the test. It never went critical.

Bohr   Thank God. Hambro and Perrin examined it after the Allied troops took over. They said it had no cadmium control rods. There was nothing to absorb any excess of neutrons, to slow the reaction down when it overheated.

Heisenberg   No rods, no.

Bohr   You believed the reaction would be self-limiting.

Heisenberg   That's what I originally believed.

Bohr   Heisenberg, the reaction would not have been self-limiting.

Heisenberg   By 1945 I understood that.

Bohr   So if you ever had got it to go critical, it would have melted down, and vanished into the centre of the earth!

Heisenberg   Not at all. We had a lump of cadmium to hand.

Bohr   A *lump* of cadmium? What were you proposing to to do with a *lump* of cadmium?

Heisenberg   Throw it into the water.

Bohr   What water?

Heisenberg   The heavy water. The moderator that the uranium was immersed in.

Bohr   My dear good Heisenberg, not to criticise, but you'd all gone mad!

Heisenberg   We were almost there! We had this fantastic neutron growth! We had 670 per cent growth!

Bohr   You'd lost all contact with reality down in that

hole!

Heisenberg Another week. Another fortnight. That's all we needed!

Bohr It was only the arrival of the Allies that saved you!

Heisenberg We'd almost reached the critical mass! A tiny bit bigger and the chain would sustain itself indefinitely. All we need is a little more uranium.
I set off with Weizsäcker to try and get our hands on Diebner's. Another hair-raising journey all the way back across Germany. Constant air raids – no trains – we try bicycles – we never make it! We end up stuck in a little inn somewhere in the middle of nowhere, listening to the thump of bombs falling all round us. And the Beethoven G minor cello sonata on the radio . . .

Bohr And everything was still under your control?

Heisenberg Under my control – yes! That's the point! Under my control!

Bohr Nothing was under anyone's control by that time!

Heisenberg Yes, because at last we were free of all constraints! The nearer the end came the faster we could work!

Bohr You were no longer running that programme, Heisenberg. The programme was running you.

Heisenberg Two more weeks, two more blocks of uranium, and it would have been German physics that achieved the world's first self-sustaining chain reaction.

Bohr Except that Fermi had already done it in Chicago, two years earlier.

Heisenberg We didn't know that.

Bohr You didn't know anything down in that cave. You were as blind as moles in a hole. Perrin said that there wasn't even anything to protect you all from the radiation.

Heisenberg We didn't have time to think about it.

Bohr So if it *had* gone critical . . .

Margrethe You'd all have died of radiation sickness.

Bohr My dear Heisenberg! My dear boy!

Heisenberg Yes, but by then the reactor would have been running.

Bohr I should have been there to look after you.

Heisenberg That's all we could think of at the time. To get the reactor running, to get the reactor running.

Bohr You always needed me there to slow you down a little. Your own walking lump of cadmium.

Heisenberg If I had died then, what should I have missed? Thirty years of attempting to explain. Thirty years of reproach and hostility. Even you turned your back on me.

Margrethe You came to Copenhagen again. You came to Tisvilde.

Heisenberg It was never the same.

Bohr No. It was never the same.

Heisenberg I sometimes think that those final few weeks at Haigerloch were the last happy time in my life. In a strange way it was very peaceful. Suddenly we were out of all the politics of Berlin. Out of the bombing. The war was coming to an end. There was nothing to think about except the reactor. And we didn't go mad, in fact. We didn't work all the time. There was a monastery on top of the rock above our cave. I used to retire to the organ-loft in the church, and play Bach fugues.

Margrethe Look at him. He's lost. He's like a lost child. He's been out in the woods all day, running here, running there. He's shown off, he's been brave, he's been cowardly.

He's done wrong, he's done right. And now the evening's come, and all he wants is to go home, and he's lost.

Heisenberg Silence.

Bohr Silence.

Margrethe Silence.

Heisenberg And once again the tiller slams over, and Christian is falling.

Bohr Once again he's struggling towards the lifebuoy.

Margrethe Once again I look up from my work, and there's Niels in the doorway, silently watching me . . .

Bohr So, Heisenberg, why did you come to Copenhagen in 1941? It was right that you told us about all the fears you had. But you didn't really think I'd tell you whether the Americans were working on a bomb.

Heisenberg No.

Bohr You didn't seriously hope that I'd stop them.

Heisenberg No.

Bohr You were going back to work on that reactor whatever I said.

Heisenberg Yes.

Bohr So, Heisenberg, why did you come?

Heisenberg Why did I come?

Bohr Tell us once again. Another draft of the paper. And this time we shall get it right. This time we shall understand.

Margrethe Maybe you'll even understand yourself.

Bohr After all, the workings of the atom were difficult to explain. We made many attempts. Each time we tried they became more obscure. We got there in the end, however. So – another draft, another draft.

Heisenberg   Why did I come? And once again I go through that evening in 1941. I crunch over the familiar gravel, and tug at the familiar bell-pull. What's in my head? Fear, certainly, and the absurd and horrible importance of someone bearing bad news. But ... yes ... something else as well. Here it comes again. I can almost see its face. Something good. Something bright and eager and hopeful.

Bohr   I open the door ...

Heisenberg   And there he is. I see his eyes light up at the sight of me.

Bohr   He's smiling his wary schoolboy smile.

Heisenberg   And I feel a moment of such consolation.

Bohr   A flash of such pure gladness.

Heisenberg   As if I'd come home after a long journey.

Bohr   As if a long-lost child had appeared on the doorstep.

Heisenberg   Suddenly I'm free of all the dark tangled currents in the water.

Bohr   Christian is alive, Harald still unborn.

Heisenberg   The world is at peace again.

Margrethe   Look at them. Father and son still. Just for a moment. Even now we're all dead.

Bohr   For a moment, yes, it's the twenties again.

Heisenberg   And we shall speak to each other and understand each other in the way we did before.

Margrethe   And from those two heads the future will emerge. Which cities will be destroyed, and which survive. Who will die, and who will live. Which world will go down to obliteration, and which will triumph.

Bohr   My dear Heisenberg!

Heisenberg   My dear Bohr!

Bohr   Come in, come in . . .

Act Two

Heisenberg It was the very beginning of spring. The first time I came to Copenhagen, in 1924. March: raw, blustery northern weather. But every now and then the sun would come out and leave that first marvellous warmth of the year on your skin. That first breath of returning life.

Bohr You were twenty-two. So I must have been . . .

Thirty-eight.

Bohr Almost the same age as you were when you came in 1941.

Heisenberg So what do we do?

Bohr Put on our boots and rucksacks . . .

Heisenberg Take the tram to the end of the line . . .

Bohr And start walking!

Heisenberg Northwards to Elsinore.

Bohr If you walk you talk.

Heisenberg Then westwards to Tisvilde.

Bohr And back by way of Hillerød.

Heisenberg Walking, talking, for a hundred miles.

Bohr After which we talked more or less non-stop for the next three years.

Heisenberg We'd split a bottle of wine over dinner in your flat at the Institute.

Bohr Then I'd come up to your room . . .

Heisenberg That terrible little room in the servants' quarters in the attic.

Bohr And we'd talk on into the small hours.

Heisenberg How, though?

Bohr How?

Heisenberg How did we talk? In Danish?

Bohr In German, surely.

Heisenberg I lectured in Danish. I had to give my first colloquium when I'd only been here for ten weeks.

Bohr I remember it. Your Danish was already excellent.

Heisenberg No. You did a terrible thing to me. Half-an-hour before it started you said casually, Oh, I think we'll speak English today.

Bohr But when you explained . . . ?

Heisenberg Explain to the Pope? I didn't dare. That excellent Danish you heard was my first attempt at English.

Bohr My dear Heisenberg! On our own together, though? My love, do you recall?

Margrethe What language you spoke when I wasn't there? You think I had microphones hidden?

Bohr No, no – but patience, my love, patience!

Margrethe Patience?

Bohr You sounded a little sharp.

Margrethe Not at all.

Bohr We have to follow the threads right back to the beginning of the maze.

Margrethe I'm watching every step.

Bohr You didn't mind? I hope.

Margrethe Mind?

Bohr Being left at home?

Margrethe While you went off on your hike? Of course not. Why should I have minded? You had to get out of the house. Two new sons arriving on top of each other would be rather a lot for any man to put up with.

Bohr   Two new sons?

Margrethe   Heisenberg.

Bohr   Yes, yes.

Margrethe   And our own son.

Bohr   Aage?

Margrethe   Ernest!

Bohr   1924 – of course – Ernest.

Margrethe   Number five. Yes?

Bohr   Yes, yes, yes. And if it was March, you're right – he couldn't have been much more than . . .

Margrethe   One week.

Bohr   One week? One week, yes. And you really didn't mind?

Margrethe   Not at all. I was pleased you had an excuse to get away. And you always went off hiking with your new assistants. You went off with Kramers, when he arrived in 1916.

Bohr   Yes, when I suppose Christian was still only . . .

Margrethe   One week.

Bohr   Yes. . . . Yes. . . . I almost killed Kramers, you know.

Heisenberg   Not with a cap-pistol?

Bohr   With a mine. On our walk.

Heisenberg   Oh, the mine. Yes, you told me, on ours. Never mind Kramers – you almost killed yourself!

Bohr   A mine washed up in the shallows . . .

Heisenberg   And of course at once they compete to

throw stones at it. What were you thinking of?

Bohr I've no idea.

Heisenberg A touch of Elsinore there, perhaps.

Bohr Elsinore?

Heisenberg The darkness inside the human soul.

Bohr You did something just as idiotic.

Heisenberg *I* did?

Bohr With Dirac in Japan. You climbed a pagoda.

Heisenberg Oh, the pagoda.

Bohr Then balanced on the pinnacle. According to Dirac. On one foot. In a high wind. I'm glad I wasn't there.

Heisenberg Elsinore, I confess.

Bohr Elsinore, certainly.

Heisenberg I was jealous of Kramers, you know.

Bohr His Eminence. Isn't that what you called him?

Heisenberg Because that's what he was. Your leading cardinal. Your favourite son. Till I arrived on the scene.

Margrethe He was a wonderful cellist.

Bohr He was a wonderful everything.

Heisenberg Far too wonderful.

Margrethe I liked him.

Heisenberg I was terrified of him. When I first started at the Institute. I was terrified of all of them. All the boy wonders you had here – they were all so brilliant and accomplished. But Kramers was the heir apparent. All the rest of us had to work in the general study hall. Kramers had the private office next to yours, like the electron on the inmost orbit around the nucleus. And he didn't think much of my physics. He insisted you could explain everything about the atom by classical mechanics.

Bohr Well, he was wrong.

Margrethe And very soon the private office was vacant.

Bohr And there was another electron on the inmost orbit.

Heisenberg Yes, and for three years we lived inside the atom.

Bohr With other electrons on the outer orbits around us all over Europe.

Heisenberg Mostly Germans.

Bohr Yes, but Schrödinger in Zürich, Fermi in Rome.

Heisenberg Chadwick and Dirac in England.

Bohr Joliot and de Broglie in Paris.

Heisenberg Gamow and Landers in Russia.

Bohr Everyone in and out of each other's departments.

Heisenberg Papers and drafts of papers on every international mail-train.

Bohr You remember when Goudsmit and Uhlenbeck did spin?

Heisenberg There's this one last variable in the quantum state of the atom that no one can make sense of. The last hurdle . . .

Bohr And these two crazy Dutchmen go back to a ridiculous idea that electrons can spin in different ways.

Heisenberg And of course the first thing that everyone wants to know is, What line is Copenhagen going to take?

Bohr I'm on my way to Leiden, as it happens.

Heisenberg And it turns into a papal progress! The train stops on the way at Hamburg . . .

Bohr Pauli and Stern are waiting on the platform to ask me what I think about spin.

Heisenberg   You tell them it's wrong.

Bohr   No, I tell them it's very . . .

Heisenberg   Interesting.

Bohr   I think that is precisely the word I choose.

Heisenberg   Then the train pulls into Leiden.

Bohr   And I'm met at the barrier by Einstein and Ehrenfest. And I change my mind because Einstein – Einstein, you see? – I'm the Pope – he's God – because Einstein has made a relativistic analysis, and it resolves all my doubts.

Heisenberg   Meanwhile I'm standing in for Born at Göttingen, so you make a detour there on your way home.

Bohr   And you and Jordan meet me at the station.

Heisenberg   Same question: what do you think of spin?

Bohr   And when the train stops at Berlin there's Pauli on the platform.

Heisenberg   Wolfgang Pauli, who never gets out of bed if he can possibly avoid it . . .

Bohr   And who's already met me once at Hamburg on the journey out . . .

Heisenberg   He's travelled all the way from Hamburg to Berlin purely in order to see you for the second time round . . .

Bohr   And find out how my ideas on spin have developed en route.

Heisenberg   Oh, those years! Those amazing years! Those three short years!

Bohr   From 1924 to 1927.

Heisenberg   From when I arrived in Copenhagen to become your assistant . . .

Bohr   To when you departed, to take up your chair at

Leipzig.

Heisenberg Three years of raw, bracing northern springtime.

Bohr At the end of which we had quantum mechanics, we had uncertainty . . .

Heisenberg We had complementarity . . .

Bohr We had the whole Copenhagen Interpretation.

Heisenberg Europe in all its glory again. A new Enlightenment, with Germany back in her rightful place at the heart of it. And who led the way for everyone else?

Margrethe You and Niels.

Heisenberg Well, we did.

Bohr We did.

Margrethe And that's what you were trying to get back to in 1941?

Heisenberg To something we did in those three years. . . . Something we said, something we thought. . . . I keep almost seeing it out of the corner of my eye as we talk! Something about the way we worked. Something about the way we did all those things . . .

Bohr Together.

Heisenberg Together. Yes, together.

Margrethe No.

Bohr No? What do you mean, no?

Margrethe Not together. You didn't do any of those things together.

Bohr Yes, we did. Of course we did.

Margrethe No, you didn't. Every single one of them you did when you were apart. *You* first worked out quantum mechanics on Heligoland. You said you couldn't think in Copenhagen.

Heisenberg   No, well, it was summer by then. I had my hay fever.

Margrethe   But on Heligoland, on your own, on a rocky bare island in the middle of the North Sea ...

Heisenberg   My head began to clear, and I had this very sharp picture of what atomic physics ought to be like. I suddenly realised that we had to limit it to the measurements we could actually make, to what we could actually observe. We can't see the electrons inside the atom ...

Margrethe   Any more than Niels can see the thoughts in your head, or you the thoughts in Niels's.

Heisenberg   All we can see are the effects that the electrons produce, on the light that they reflect ...

Bohr   But the difficulties you were trying to resolve were the ones we'd explored together, over dinner in the flat, on the beach at Tisvilde.

Heisenberg   Of course. But I remember the evening when the mathematics first began to chime with the principle.

Margrethe   On Heligoland.

Heisenberg   On Heligoland.

Margrethe   On your own.

Heisenberg   It was terribly laborious – I didn't understand matrix calculus then – no one did – it was a very obscure backwater of arithmetic ... I get so excited I keep making mistakes. But by three in the morning I've got it. I seem to be looking through the surface of atomic phenomena into a strangely beautiful interior world. A world of pure mathematical structures. I'm too excited to sleep. I go down to the southern end of the island. There's a rock jutting out into the sea that I've been longing to climb. I get up it in the half-light before the dawn, and lie on top, gazing out to sea.

Margrethe On your own.

Heisenberg On my own. And yes – I was happy.

Margrethe Happier than you were back here with us all in Copenhagen the following winter.

Heisenberg What, with all the Schrödinger nonsense?

Bohr Nonsense? Come, come. Schrödinger's wave formulation?

Margrethe Yes, suddenly everyone's turned their backs on your wonderful new matrix mechanics.

Heisenberg No one can understand it.

Margrethe And they *can* understand Schrödinger's wave mechanics.

Heisenberg Because they'd learnt it in school! We're going backwards to classical physics! And when I'm a little cautious about accepting it . . .

Bohr A little cautious? Not to criticise, but . . .

Margrethe . . . You described it as repulsive!

Heisenberg I said the physical implications were repulsive. Schrödinger said my mathematics were repulsive.

Bohr I seem to recall you used the word . . . well, I won't repeat it in mixed company.

Heisenberg In private. But by that time people had gone crazy.

Margrethe They thought you were simply jealous.

Heisenberg Someone even suggested some bizarre kind of intellectual snobbery. You got extremely excited.

Bohr On your behalf.

Heisenberg You invited Schrödinger here . . .

Bohr   To have a calm debate about our differences.

Heisenberg   And you fell on him like a madman. You meet him at the station – of course – and you pitch into him before he's even got his bags off the train. Then you go on at him from first thing in the morning until last thing at night.

Bohr   *I* go on? *He* goes on!

Heisenberg   Because you won't make the least concession!

Bohr   Nor will he!

Heisenberg   You made him ill! He had to retire to bed to get away from you!

Bohr   He had a slight feverish cold.

Heisenberg   Margrethe had to nurse him!

Margrethe   I dosed him with tea and cake to keep his strength up.

Heisenberg   Yes, while you pursued him even into the sickroom! Sat on his bed and hammered away at him!

Bohr   Perfectly politely.

Heisenberg   You were the Pope and the Holy Office and the Inquisition all rolled into one! And then, and then, after Schrödinger had fled back to Zürich – and this I will never forget, Bohr, this I will never let you forget – you started to take his side! You turned on me!

Bohr   Because *you'd* gone mad by this time! You'd become fanatical! You were refusing to allow wave theory any place in quantum mechanics at all!

Heisenberg   You'd completely turned your coat!

Bohr   I said wave mechanics and matrix mechanics were simply alternative tools.

Heisenberg   Something you're always accusing me of. 'If it works it works.' Never mind what it means.

Bohr   Of course I mind what it means.

Heisenberg   What it means in language.

Bohr   In plain language, yes.

Heisenberg   What something means is what it means in mathematics.

Bohr   You think that so long as the mathematics works out, the sense doesn't matter.

Heisenberg   Mathematics *is* sense! That's what sense is!

Bohr   But in the end, in the end, remember, we have to be able to explain it all to Margrethe!

Margrethe   Explain it to me? You couldn't even explain it to each other! You went on arguing into the small hours every night! You both got so angry!

Bohr   We also both got completely exhausted.

Margrethe   It was the cloud chamber that finished you.

Bohr   Yes, because if you detach an electron from an atom, and send it through a cloud chamber, you can see the track it leaves.

Heisenberg   And it's a scandal. There shouldn't be a track!

Margrethe   According to your quantum mechanics.

Heisenberg   There *isn't* a track! No orbits! No tracks or trajectories! Only external effects!

Margrethe   Only there the track is. I've seen it myself, as clear as the wake left by a passing ship.

Bohr   It was a fascinating paradox.

Heisenberg   You actually loved the paradoxes, that's your problem. You revelled in the contradictions.

Bohr   Yes, and you've never been able to understand the suggestiveness of paradox and contradiction. That's *your* problem. You live and breathe paradox and contradiction, but you can no more see the beauty of them than the fish can see the beauty of the water.

Heisenberg I sometimes felt as if I was trapped in a kind of windowless hell. You don't realise how aggressive you are. Prowling up and down the room as if you're going to eat someone – and I can guess who it's going to be.

Bohr That's the way we did the physics, though.

Margrethe No. No! In the end you did it on your own again! Even you! You went off ski-ing in Norway.

Bohr I had to get away from it all!

Margrethe And you worked out complementarity in Norway, on your own.

Heisenberg The speed he skis at he had to do *something* to keep the blood going round. It was either physics or frostbite.

Bohr Yes, and you stayed behind in Copenhagen . . .

Heisenberg And started to think at last.

Margrethe You're a lot better off apart, you two.

Heisenberg Having him out of town was as liberating as getting away from my hay fever on Heligoland.

Margrethe I shouldn't let you sit anywhere near each other, if I were the teacher.

Heisenberg And that's when I did uncertainty. Walking round Faelled Park on my own one horrible raw February night. It's very late, and as soon as I've turned off into the park I'm completely alone in the darkness. I start to think about what you'd see, if you could train a telescope on me from the mountains of Norway. You'd see me by the street-lamps on the Blegdamsvej, then nothing as I vanished into the darkness, then another glimpse of me as I passed the lamp-post in front of the bandstand. And that's what we see in the cloud chamber. Not a continuous track but a series of glimpses – a series of collisions between the

passing electron and various atoms of water vapour. . . . Or
think of you, on your great papal progress to Leiden in
1925. What did Margrethe see of that, at home here in
Copenhagen? A picture postcard from Hamburg, perhaps.
Then one from Leiden. One from Göttingen. One from
Berlin. Because what we see in the cloud chamber are not
even the collisions themselves, but the water-droplets that
condense around them, as big as cities around a traveller –
no, vastly bigger still, relatively – complete countries –
Germany . . . Holland . . . Germany again. There is no
track, there are no precise addresses; only a vague list of
countries visited. I don't know why we hadn't thought of it
before, except that we were too busy arguing to think at
all.

Bohr You seem to have given up on all forms of
discussion. By the time I get back from Norway I find
you've done a draft of your uncertainty paper and you've
already sent it for publication!

Margrethe And an even worse battle begins.

Bohr My dear good Heisenberg, it's not open behaviour
to rush a first draft into print before we've discussed it
together! It's not the way we work!

Heisenberg No, the way we work is that you hound me
from first thing in the morning till last thing at night! The
way we work is that you drive me mad!

Bohr Yes, because the paper contains a fundamental
error.

Margrethe And here we go again.

Heisenberg No, but I show him the strangest truth
about the universe that any of us has stumbled on since
relativity – that you can never know everything about the
whereabouts of a particle, or anything else, even Bohr now,
as he prowls up and down the room in that maddening
way of his, because we can't observe it without introducing
some new element into the situation, an atom of water
vapour for it to hit, or a piece of light – things which have

an energy of their own, and which therefore have an effect on what they hit. A small one, admittedly, in the case of Bohr . . .

Bohr   Yes, if you know where I am with the kind of accuracy we're talking about when we're dealing with particles, you can still measure my velocity to within – what . . .?

Heisenberg   Something like a billionth of a billionth of a kilometre per second. The theoretical point remains, though, that you have no absolutely determinate situation in the world, which among other things lays waste to the idea of causality, the whole foundation of science – because if you don't know how things are today you certainly can't know how they're going to be tomorrow. I shatter the objective universe around you – and all you can say is that there's an error in the formulation!

Bohr   There is!

Margrethe   Tea, anyone? Cake?

Heisenberg   Listen, in my paper what we're trying to locate is not a free electron off on its travels through a cloud chamber, but an electron when it's at home, moving around inside an atom . . .

Bohr   And the uncertainty arises not, as you claim, through its indeterminate recoil when it's hit by an incoming photon . . .

Heisenberg   Plain language, plain language!

Bohr   This *is* plain language.

Heisenberg   Listen . . .

Bohr   The language of classical mechanics.

Heisenberg   Listen! Copenhagen is an atom. Margrethe is its nucleus. About right, the scale? Ten thousand to one?

Bohr   Yes, yes.

Heisenberg   Now, Bohr's an electron. He's wandering

about the city somewhere in the darkness, no one knows
where. He's here, he's there, he's everywhere and nowhere.
Up in Faelled Park, down at Carlsberg. Passing City Hall,
out by the harbour. I'm a photon. A quantum of light. I'm
despatched into the darkness to find Bohr. And I succeed,
because I manage to collide with him. . . . But what's
happened? Look – he's been slowed down, he's been
deflected! He's no longer doing exactly what he was so
maddeningly doing when I walked into him!

Bohr   But, Heisenberg, Heisenberg! You also have been
deflected! If people can see what's happened to you, to
their piece of light, then they can work out what must have
happened to me! The trouble is knowing what's happened
to you! Because to understand how people see you we have
to treat you not just as a particle, but as a wave. I have to
use not only your particle mechanics, I have to use the
Schrödinger wave function.

Heisenberg   I know – I put it in a postscript to my
paper.

Bohr   Everyone remembers the paper – no one
remembers the postscript. But the question is fundamental.
Particles are things, complete in themselves. Waves are
disturbances in something else.

Heisenberg   I know. Complementarity. It's in the
postscript.

Bohr   They're either one thing or the other. They can't
be both. We have to choose one way of seeing them or the
other. But as soon as we do we can't know everything
about them.

Heisenberg   And off he goes into orbit again.
Incidentally exemplifying another application of
complementarity. Exactly where you go as you ramble
around is of course completely determined by your genes
and the various physical forces acting on you. But it's also
completely determined by your own entirely inscrutable
whims from one moment to the next. So we can't

completely understand your behaviour without seeing it both ways at once, and that's impossible. Which means that your extraordinary peregrinations are not fully objective aspects of the universe. They exist only partially, through the efforts of me or Margrethe, as our minds shift endlessly back and forth between the two approaches.

Bohr You've never absolutely and totally accepted complementarity, have you?

Heisenberg Yes! Absolutely and totally! I defended it at the Como Conference in 1927! I have adhered to it ever afterwards with religious fervour! You convinced me. I humbly accepted your criticisms.

Bohr Not before you'd said some deeply wounding things.

Heisenberg Good God, at one point you literally reduced me to tears!

Bohr Forgive me, but I diagnosed them as tears of frustration and rage.

Heisenberg I was having a tantrum?

Bohr I have brought up children of my own.

Heisenberg And what about Margrethe? Was *she* having a tantrum? Klein told me you reduced *her* to tears after I'd gone, making her type out your endless redraftings of the complementarity paper.

Bohr I don't recall that.

Margrethe I do.

Heisenberg We had to drag Pauli out of bed in Hamburg once again to come to Copenhagen and negotiate peace.

Bohr He succeeded. We ended up with a treaty. Uncertainty and complementarity became the two central tenets of the Copenhagen Interpretation of Quantum Mechanics.

Heisenberg A political compromise, of course, like most treaties.

Bohr You see? Somewhere inside you there are still secret reservations.

Heisenberg Not at all – it works. That's what matters. It works, it works, it works!

Bohr It works, yes. But it's more important than that. Because you see what we did in those three years, Heisenberg? Not to exaggerate, but we turned the world inside out! Yes, listen, now it comes, now it comes. . . . We put man back at the centre of the universe. Throughout history we keep finding ourselves displaced. We keep exiling ourselves to the periphery of things. First we turn ourselves into a mere adjunct of God's unknowable purposes, tiny figures kneeling in the great cathedral of creation. And no sooner have we recovered ourselves in the Renaissance, no sooner has man become, as Protagoras proclaimed him, the measure of all things, than we're pushed aside again by the products of our own reasoning! We're dwarfed again as physicists build the great new cathedrals for us to wonder at – the laws of classical mechanics that predate us from the beginning of eternity, that will survive us to eternity's end, that exist whether we exist or not. Until we come to the beginning of the twentieth century, and we're suddenly forced to rise from our knees again.

Heisenberg It starts with Einstein.

Bohr It starts with Einstein. He shows that measurement – measurement, on which the whole possibility of science depends – measurement is not an impersonal event that occurs with impartial universality. It's a human act, carried out from a specific point of view in time and space, from the one particular viewpoint of a possible observer. Then, here in Copenhagen in those three years in the mid-twenties we discover that there is no precisely determinable objective universe. That the universe exists only as a series of approximations. Only within the limits determined by our relationship with it. Only through the understanding lodged inside the human head.

Margrethe So this man you've put at the centre of the universe – is it you, or is it Heisenberg?

Bohr Now, now, my love.

Margrethe Yes, but it makes a difference.

Bohr Either of us. Both of us. Yourself. All of us.

Margrethe If it's Heisenberg at the centre of the universe, then the one bit of the universe that he can't see is Heisenberg.

Heisenberg So . . .

Margrethe So it's no good asking him why he came to Copenhagen in 1941. He doesn't know!

Heisenberg I thought for a moment just then I caught a glimpse of it.

Margrethe Then you turned to look.

Heisenberg And away it went.

Margrethe Complementarity again. Yes?

Bohr Yes, yes.

Margrethe I've typed it out often enough. If you're doing something you have to concentrate on you can't also be thinking about doing it, and if you're thinking about doing it then you can't actually be doing it. Yes?

Heisenberg Swerve left, swerve right, or think about it and die.

Bohr But *after* you've done it . . .

Margrethe You look back and make a guess, just like the rest of us. Only a worse guess, because you didn't see yourself doing it, and we did. Forgive me, but you don't even know why you did uncertainty in the first place.

Bohr Whereas if *you're* the one at the centre of the universe . . .

Margrethe Then I can tell you that it was because you wanted to drop a bomb on Schrödinger.

Heisenberg I wanted to show he was wrong, certainly.

Margrethe And Schrödinger was winning the war. When the Leipzig chair first became vacant that autumn he was short-listed for it and you weren't. You needed a wonderful new weapon.

Bohr Not to criticise, Margrethe, but you have a tendency to make everything personal.

Margrethe Because everything *is* personal! You've just read us all a lecture about it! You know how much Heisenberg wanted a chair. You know the pressure he was under from his family. I'm sorry, but you want to make everything seem heroically abstract and logical. And when you tell the story, yes, it all falls into place, it all has a beginning and a middle and an end. But I was there, and when I remember what it was like I'm there still, and I look around me and what I see isn't a story! It's confusion and rage and jealousy and tears and no one knowing what things mean or which way they're going to go.

Heisenberg All the same, it works, it works.

Margrethe Yes, it works wonderfully. Within three months of publishing your uncertainty paper you're offered Leipzig.

Heisenberg I didn't mean that.

Margrethe Not to mention somewhere else and somewhere else.

Heisenberg Halle and Munich and Zürich.

Bohr And various American universities.

Heisenberg But I didn't mean that.

Margrethe And when you take up your chair at Leipzig you're how old?

Heisenberg Twenty-six.

Bohr The youngest full professor in Germany.

Heisenberg I mean the Copenhagen Interpretation. The Copenhagen Interpretation works. However we got there, by whatever combination of high principles and low calculation, of most painfully hard thought and most painfully childish tears, it works. It goes on working.

Margrethe Yes, and why did you both accept the Interpretation in the end? Was it really because you wanted to re-establish humanism?

Bohr Of course not. It was because it was the only way to explain what the experimenters had observed.

Margrethe Or was it because now you were becoming a professor you wanted a solidly established doctrine to teach? Because you wanted to have your new ideas publicly endorsed by the head of the church in Copenhagen? And perhaps Niels agreed to endorse them in return for your accepting *his* doctrines. For recognising him as head of the church. And if you want to know why you came to Copenhagen in 1941 I'll tell you that as well. You're right – there's no great mystery about it. You came to show yourself off to us.

Bohr Margrethe!

Margrethe No! When he first came in 1924 he was a humble assistant lecturer from a humiliated nation, grateful to have a job. Now here you are, back in triumph – the leading scientist in a nation that's conquered most of Europe. You've come to show us how well you've done in life.

Bohr This is so unlike you!

Margrethe I'm sorry, but isn't that really why he's here? Because he's burning to let us know that he's in charge of some vital piece of secret research. And that even so he's preserved a lofty moral independence. Preserved it so famously that he's being watched by the Gestapo. Preserved it so successfully that he's now also got a wonderfully important moral dilemma to face.

Bohr   Yes, well, now you're simply working yourself up.

Margrethe   A chain reaction. You tell one painful truth and it leads to two more. And as you frankly admit, you're going to go back and continue doing precisely what you were doing before, whatever Niels tells you.

Heisenberg   Yes.

Margrethe   Because you wouldn't dream of giving up such a wonderful opportunity for research.

Heisenberg   Not if I can possibly help it.

Margrethe   Also you want to demonstrate to the Nazis how useful theoretical physics can be. You want to save the honour of German science. You want to be there to re-establish it in all its glory as soon as the war's over.

Heisenberg   All the same, I don't tell Speer that the reactor . . .

Margrethe   . . . will produce plutonium, no, because you're afraid of what will happen if the Nazis commit huge resources, and you fail to deliver the bombs. Please don't try to tell us that you're a hero of the resistance.

Heisenberg   I've never claimed to be a hero.

Margrethe   Your talent is for ski-ing too fast for anyone to see where you are. For always being in more than one position at a time, like one of your particles.

Heisenberg   I can only say that it worked. Unlike most of the gestures made by heroes of the resistance. It worked! I know what you think. You think I should have joined the plot against Hitler, and got myself hanged like the others.

Bohr   Of course not.

Heisenberg You don't say it, because there are some things that can't be said. But you think it.

Bohr No.

Heisenberg What would it have achieved? What would it have achieved if you'd dived in after Christian, and drowned as well? But that's another thing that can't be said.

Bohr Only thought.

Heisenberg Yes. I'm sorry.

Bohr And rethought. Every day.

Heisenberg You had to be held back, I know.

Margrethe Whereas you held yourself back.

Heisenberg Better to stay on the boat, though, and fetch it about. Better to remain alive, and throw the lifebuoy. Surely!

Bohr Perhaps. Perhaps not.

Heisenberg Better. Better.

Margrethe Really it is ridiculous. You reasoned your way, both of you, with such astonishing delicacy and precision into the tiny world of the atom. Now it turns out that everything depends upon these really rather large objects on our shoulders. And what's going on in there is . . .

Heisenberg Elsinore.

Margrethe Elsinore, yes.

Heisenberg And you may be right. I *was* afraid of what would happen. I *was* conscious of being on the winning side. . . So many explanations for everything I did! So many of them sitting round the lunch-table! Somewhere

at the head of the table, I think, is the real reason I came
to Copenhagen. Again I turn to look. . . . And for a
moment I almost see its face. Then next time I look the
chair at the head of the table is completely empty. There's
no reason at all. I didn't tell Speer simply because I didn't
think of it. I came to Copenhagen simply because I did
think of it. A million things we might do or might not do
every day. A million decisions that make themselves.

Bohr   Why didn't I . . . ?

Heisenberg   Kill me. Murder me. That evening in 1941.
Here we are, walking back towards the house, and you've
just leapt to the conclusion that I'm going to arm Hitler
with nuclear weapons. You'll surely take any reasonable
steps to prevent it happening.

Bohr   By murdering you?

Heisenberg   We're in the middle of a war. I'm an
enemy. There's nothing odd or immoral about killing
enemies.

Bohr   I should fetch out my cap-pistol?

Heisenberg   You won't need your cap-pistol. You won't
even need a mine. You can do it without any loud bangs,
without any blood, without any spectacle of suffering. As
cleanly as a bomb-aimer pressing his release three thousand
metres above the earth. You simply wait till I've gone.
Then you sit quietly down in your favourite armchair here
and repeat aloud to Margrethe, in front of our unseen
audience, what I've just told you. I shall be dead almost as
soon as poor Casimir. A lot sooner than Gamow.

Bohr   My dear Heisenberg, the suggestion is of course . . .

Heisenberg   Most interesting. So interesting that it never
even occurred to you. Complementarity, once again. I'm
your enemy; I'm also your friend. I'm a danger to

mankind; I'm also your guest. I'm a particle; I'm also a wave. We have one set of obligations to the world in general, and we have other sets, never to be reconciled, to our fellow-countrymen, to our neighbours, to our friends, to our family, to our children. We have to go through not two slits at the same time but twenty-two. All we can do is to look afterwards, and see what happened.

Margrethe   I'll tell you another reason why you did uncertainty: you have a natural affinity for it.

Heisenberg   Well, I must cut a gratifyingly chastened figure when I return in 1947. Crawling on my hands and knees again. My nation back in ruins.

Margrethe   Not really. You're demonstrating that once more you personally have come out on top.

Heisenberg   Begging for food parcels?

Margrethe   Established in Göttingen under British protection, in charge of post-war German science.

Heisenberg   That first year in Göttingen I slept on straw.

Margrethe   Elisabeth said you had a most charming house thereafter.

Heisenberg   I was given it by the British.

Margrethe   Your new foster-parents. Who'd confiscated it from someone else.

Bohr   Enough, my love, enough.

Margrethe   No, I've kept my thoughts to myself for all these years. But it's maddening to have this clever son forever dancing about in front of our eyes, forever demanding our approval, forever struggling to shock us, forever begging to be told what the limits to his freedom are, if only so that he can go out and transgress them! I'm sorry, but really. . . . On your hands and knees? It's my dear, good, kind husband who's on his hands and knees! Literally. Crawling down to the beach in the darkness in

1943, fleeing like a thief in the night from his own homeland to escape being murdered. The protection of the German Embassy that you boasted about didn't last for long. We were incorporated into the Reich.

Heisenberg I warned you in 1941. You wouldn't listen. At least Bohr got across to Sweden.

Margrethe And even as the fishing-boat was taking him across the Sound two freighters were arriving in the harbour to ship the entire Jewish population of Denmark eastwards. That great darkness inside the human soul was flooding out to engulf us all.

Heisenberg I did try to warn you.

Margrethe Yes, and where are you? Shut away in a cave like a savage, trying to conjure an evil spirit out of a hole in the ground. That's what it came down to in the end, all that shining springtime in the 1920s, that's what it produced – a more efficient machine for killing people.

Bohr It breaks my heart every time I think of it.

Heisenberg It broke all our hearts.

Margrethe And this wonderful machine may yet kill every man, woman, and child in the world. And if we really are the centre of the universe, if we really are all that's keeping it in being, what will be left?

Bohr Darkness. Total and final darkness.

Margrethe Even the questions that haunt us will at last be extinguished. Even the ghosts will die.

Heisenberg I can only say that I didn't do it. I didn't build the bomb.

Margrethe No, and why didn't you? I'll tell you that, too. It's the simplest reason of all. Because you couldn't. You didn't understand the physics.

Heisenberg That's what Goudsmit said.

Margrethe And Goudsmit knew. He was one of your

magic circle. He and Uhlenbeck were the ones who did spin.

Heisenberg All the same, he had no idea of what I did or didn't understand about a bomb.

Margrethe He tracked you down across Europe for Allied Intelligence. He interrogated you after you were captured.

Heisenberg He blamed me, of course. His parents died in Auschwitz. He thought I should have done something to save them. I don't know what. So many hands stretching up from the darkness for a lifeline, and no lifeline that could ever reach them . . .

Margrethe He said you didn't understand the crucial difference between a reactor and a bomb.

Heisenberg I understood very clearly. I simply didn't tell the others.

Margrethe Ah.

Heisenberg I understood, though.

Margrethe But secretly.

Heisenberg You can check if you don't believe me.

Margrethe There's evidence, for once?

Heisenberg It was all most carefully recorded.

Margrethe Witnesses, even?

Heisenberg Unimpeachable witnesses.

Margrethe Who wrote it down?

Heisenberg Who recorded it and transcribed it.

Margrethe Even though you didn't tell anyone?

Heisenberg I told one person. I told Otto Hahn. That terrible night at Farm Hall, after we'd heard the news. Somewhere in the small hours, after everyone had finally gone to bed, and we were alone together. I gave him a reasonably good account of how the bomb had worked.

Margrethe   After the event.

Heisenberg   After the event. Yes. When it didn't matter any more. All the things Goudsmit said I didn't understand. Fast neutrons in 235. The plutonium option. A reflective shell to reduce neutron escape. Even the method of triggering it.

Bohr   The critical mass. That was the most important thing. The amount of material you needed to establish the chain-reaction. Did you tell him the critical mass?

Heisenberg   I gave him a figure, yes. You can look it up! Because that was the other secret of the house-party. Diebner asked me when we first arrived if I thought there were hidden microphones. I laughed. I told him the British were far too old-fashioned to know about Gestapo methods. I underestimated them. They had microphones everywhere – they were recording everything. Look it up! Everything we said. Everything we went through that terrible night. Everything I told Hahn alone in the small hours.

Bohr   But the critical mass. You gave him a figure. What was the figure you gave him?

Heisenberg   I forget.

Bohr   Heisenberg . . .

Heisenberg   It's all on the record. You can see for yourself.

Bohr   The figure for the Hiroshima bomb . . .

Heisenberg   Was fifty kilograms.

Bohr   So that was the figure you gave Hahn? Fifty kilograms?

Heisenberg   I said about a ton.

Bohr   About a ton? A thousand kilograms? Heisenberg, I believe I am at last beginning to understand something.

Heisenberg   The one thing I was wrong about.

Bohr   You were twenty times over.

Heisenberg   The one thing.

Bohr   But, Heisenberg, your mathematics, your mathematics! How could they have been so far out?

Heisenberg   They weren't. As soon as I calculated the diffusion I got it just about right.

Bohr   As soon as you calculated it?

Heisenberg   I gave everyone a seminar on it a week later. It's in the record! Look it up!

Bohr   You mean . . . you hadn't calculated it before? You hadn't done the diffusion equation?

Heisenberg   There was no need to.

Bohr   No need to?

Heisenberg   The calculation had already been done.

Bohr   Done by whom?

Heisenberg   By Perrin and Flügge in 1939.

Bohr   By Perrin and Flügge? But, my dear Heisenberg, that was for natural uranium. Wheeler and I showed that it was only the 235 that fissioned.

Heisenberg   Your great paper. The basis of everything we did.

Bohr   So you needed to calculate the figure for pure 235.

Heisenberg   Obviously.

Bohr   And you didn't?

Heisenberg   I didn't.

Bohr   And that's why you were so confident you couldn't do it until you had the plutonium. Because you spent the entire war believing that it would take not a few kilograms of 235, but a ton or more. And to make a ton of 235 in any plausible time . . .

Heisenberg Would have needed something like two hundred million separator units. It was plainly unimaginable.

Bohr If you'd realised you had to produce only a few kilograms . . .

Heisenberg Even to make a single kilogram would need something like two hundred thousand units.

Bohr But two hundred million is one thing; two hundred thousand is another. You might just possibly have imagined setting up two hundred thousand.

Heisenberg Just possibly.

Bohr The Americans did imagine it.

Heisenberg Because Otto Frisch and Rudolf Peierls actually did the calculation. They solved the diffusion equation.

Bohr Frisch was my old assistant.

Heisenberg Peierls was my old pupil.

Bohr An Austrian and a German.

Heisenberg So they should have been making their calculation for us, at the Kaiser Wilhelm Institute in Berlin. But instead they made it at the University of Birmingham, in England.

Margrethe Because they were Jews.

Heisenberg There's something almost mathematically elegant about that.

Bohr They also started with Perrin and Flügge.

Heisenberg They also thought it would take tons. They also thought it was unimaginable.

Bohr Until one day . . .

Heisenberg They did the calculation.

Bohr They discovered just how fast the chain reaction

would go.

Heisenberg   And therefore how little material you'd need.

Bohr   They said slightly over half a kilogram.

Heisenberg   About the size of a tennis ball.

Bohr   They were wrong, of course.

Heisenberg   They were ten times under.

Bohr   Which made it seem ten times more imaginable than it actually was.

Heisenberg   Whereas I left it seeming twenty times less imaginable.

Bohr   So all your agonising in Copenhagen about plutonium was beside the point. You could have done it without ever building the reactor. You could have done it with 235 all the time.

Heisenberg   Almost certainly not.

Bohr   Just possibly, though.

Heisenberg   Just possibly.

Bohr   And *that* question you'd settled long before you arrived in Copenhagen. Simply by failing to try the diffusion equation.

Heisenberg   Such a tiny failure.

Bohr   But the consequences went branching out over the years, doubling and redoubling.

Heisenberg   Until they were large enough to save a city. Which city? Any of the cities that we never dropped our bomb on.

Bohr   London, presumably, if you'd had it in time. If the Americans had already entered the war, and the Allies had begun to liberate Europe, then . . .

Heisenberg   Who knows? Paris as well. Amsterdam.

Perhaps Copenhagen.

Bohr   So, Heisenberg, tell us this one simple thing: why didn't you do the calculation?

Heisenberg   The question is why Frisch and Peierls *did* do it. It was a stupid waste of time. However much 235 it turned out to be, it was obviously going to be more than anyone could imagine producing.

Bohr   Except that it wasn't!

Heisenberg   Except that it wasn't.

Bohr   So why . . . ?

Heisenberg   I don't know! I don't know why I didn't do it! Because I never thought of it! Because it didn't occur to me! Because I assumed it wasn't worth doing!

Bohr   Assumed? Assumed? You never assumed things! That's how you got uncertainty, because you rejected our assumptions! You calculated, Heisenberg! You calculated everything! The first thing you did with a problem was the mathematics!

Heisenberg   You should have been there to slow me down.

Bohr   Yes, you wouldn't have got away with it if I'd been standing over you.

Heisenberg   Though in fact you made exactly the same assumption! You thought there was no danger for exactly the same reason as I did! Why didn't *you* calculate it?

Bohr   Why didn't *I* calculate it?

Heisenberg   Tell us why *you* didn't calculate it and we'll know why *I* didn't!

Bohr   It's obvious why *I* didn't!

Heisenberg   Go on.

Margrethe   Because he wasn't trying to build a bomb!

Heisenberg   Yes. Thank you. Because he wasn't trying to build a bomb. I imagine it was the same with me. Because *I* wasn't trying to build a bomb. Thank you.

Bohr   So, you bluffed yourself, the way I did at poker with the straight I never had. But in that case . . .

Heisenberg   Why did I come to Copenhagen? Yes, why did I come . . . ?

Bohr   One more draft, yes? One final draft!

Heisenberg   And once again I crunch over the familiar gravel to the Bohrs' front door, and tug at the familiar bell-pull. Why have I come? I know perfectly well. Know so well that I've no need to ask myself. Until once again the heavy front door opens.

Bohr   He stands on the doorstep blinking in the sudden flood of light from the house. Until this instant his thoughts have been everywhere and nowhere, like unobserved particles, through all the slits in the diffraction grating simultaneously. Now they have to be observed and specified.

Heisenberg   And at once the clear purposes inside my head lose all definite shape. The light falls on them and they scatter.

Bohr   My dear Heisenberg!

Heisenberg   My dear Bohr!

Bohr   Come in, come in . . .

Heisenberg   How difficult it is to see even what's in front of one's eyes. All we possess is the present, and the present endlessly dissolves into the past. Bohr has gone even as I turn to see Margrethe.

Margrethe   Niels is right. You look older.

Bohr   I believe you had some personal trouble.

Heisenberg   Margrethe slips into history even as I turn back to Bohr. And yet how much more difficult still it is to

catch the slightest glimpse of what's behind one's eyes.
Here I am at the centre of the universe, and yet all I can
see are two smiles that don't belong to me.

Margrethe How is Elisabeth? How are the children?

Heisenberg Very well. They send their love, of course
... I can feel a third smile in the room, very close to me.
Could it be the one I suddenly see for a moment in the
mirror there? And is the awkward stranger wearing it in
any way connected with this presence that I can feel in the
room? This all-enveloping, unobserved presence?

Margrethe I watch the two smiles in the room, one
awkward and ingratiating, the other rapidly fading from
incautious warmth to bare politeness. There's also a third
smile in the room, I know, unchangingly courteous, I hope,
and unchangingly guarded.

Heisenberg You've managed to get some ski-ing?

Bohr I glance at Margrethe, and for a moment I see
what she can see and I can't – myself, and the smile
vanishing from my face as poor Heisenberg blunders on.

Heisenberg I look at the two of them looking at me,
and for a moment I see the third person in the room as
clearly as I see them. Their importunate guest, stumbling
from one crass and unwelcome thoughtfulness to the next.

Bohr I look at him looking at me, anxiously, pleadingly,
urging me back to the old days, and I see what he sees.
And yes – now it comes, now it comes – there's someone
missing from the room. He sees me. He sees Margrethe.
He doesn't see himself.

Heisenberg Two thousand million people in the world,
and the one who has to decide their fate is the only one
who's always hidden from me.

Bohr You suggested a stroll.

Heisenberg You remember Elsinore? The darkness inside the human soul . . . ?

Bohr And out we go. Out under the autumn trees. Through the blacked-out streets.

Heisenberg Now there's no one in the world except Bohr and the invisible other. Who is he, this all-enveloping presence in the darkness?

Margrethe The flying particle wanders the darkness, no one knows where. It's here, it's there, it's everywhere and nowhere.

Bohr With careful casualness he begins to ask the question he's prepared.

Heisenberg Does one as a physicist have the moral right to work on the practical exploitation of atomic energy?

Margrethe The great collision.

Bohr I stop. He stops . . .

Margrethe This is how they work.

Heisenberg He gazes at me, horrified.

Margrethe Now at last he knows where he is and what he's doing.

Heisenberg He turns away.

Margrethe And even as the moment of collision begins it's over.

Bohr Already we're hurrying back towards the house.

Margrethe Already they're both flying away from each other into the darkness again.

Heisenberg Our conversation's over.

Bohr Our great partnership.

Heisenberg All our friendship.

Margrethe   And everything about him becomes as uncertain as it was before.

Bohr   Unless . . . yes . . . a thought-experiment. . . . Let's suppose for a moment that I don't go flying off into the night. Let's see what happens if instead I remember the paternal role I'm supposed to play. If I stop, and control my anger, and turn to him. And ask him why.

Heisenberg   Why?

Bohr   Why are you confident that it's going to be so reassuringly difficult to build a bomb with 235? Is it because you've done the calculation?

Heisenberg   The calculation?

Bohr   Of the diffusion in 235. No. It's because you haven't calculated it. You haven't considered calculating it. You hadn't consciously realised there was a calculation to be made.

Heisenberg   And of course now I *have* realised. In fact it wouldn't be all that difficult. Let's see. . . . The scattering cross-section's about 6×10^{-24}, so the mean free path would be . . . Hold on . . .

Bohr   And suddenly a very different and very terrible new world begins to take shape . . .

Margrethe   That was the last and greatest demand that Heisenberg made on his friendship with you. To be understood when he couldn't understand himself. And that was the last and greatest act of friendship for Heisenberg that you performed in return. To leave him misunderstood.

Heisenberg   Yes. Perhaps I should thank you.

Bohr   Perhaps you should.

Margrethe   Anyway, it was the end of the story.

Bohr   Though perhaps there was also something I should thank *you* for. That summer night in 1943, when I escaped across the Sound in the fishing-boat, and the freighters arrived from Germany . . .

Margrethe   What's that to do with Heisenberg?

Bohr   When the ships arrived on the Wednesday there were eight thousand Jews in Denmark to be arrested and crammed into their holds. On the Friday evening, at the start of the Sabbath, when the SS began their round-up, there was scarcely a Jew to be found.

Margrethe   They'd all been hidden in churches and hospitals, in people's homes and country cottages.

Bohr   But how was that possible? – Because we'd been tipped off by someone in the German Embassy.

Heisenberg   Georg Duckwitz, their shipping specialist.

Bohr   Your man?

Heisenberg   One of them.

Bohr   He was a remarkable informant. He told us the day before the freighters arrived – the very day that Hitler issued the order. He gave us the exact time that the SS would move.

Margrethe   It was the Resistance who got them out of their hiding-places and smuggled them across the Sound.

Bohr   For a handful of us in one fishing smack to get past the German patrol-boats was remarkable enough. For a whole armada to get past, with the best part of eight thousand people on board, was like the Red Sea parting.

Margrethe   I thought there *were* no German patrol-boats that night?

Bohr   No – the whole squadron had suddenly been reported unseaworthy.

Heisenberg   How they got away with it I can't imagine.

Bohr   Duckwitz again?

Heisenberg   He also went to Stockholm and asked the Swedish Government to accept everyone.

Bohr   So perhaps I should thank you.

Heisenberg   For what?

Bohr   My life. All our lives.

Heisenberg   Nothing to do with me by that time. I regret to say.

Bohr   But after I'd gone you came back to Copenhagen.

Heisenberg   To make sure that our people didn't take over the Institute in your absence.

Bohr   I've never thanked you for that, either.

Heisenberg   You know they offered me your cyclotron?

Bohr   You could have separated a little 235 with it.

Heisenberg   Meanwhile you were going on from Sweden to Los Alamos.

Bohr   To play my small but helpful part in the deaths of a hundred thousand people.

Margrethe   Niels, you did nothing wrong!

Bohr   Didn't I?

Heisenberg   Of course not. You were a good man, from first to last, and no one could ever say otherwise. Whereas I . . .

Bohr   Whereas you, my dear Heisenberg, never managed to contribute to the death of one single solitary person in all your life.

Margrethe   Well, yes.

Heisenberg   Did I?

Margrethe   One. Or so you told us. The poor fellow you guarded overnight, when you were a boy in Munich, while he was waiting to be shot in the morning.

Bohr   All right then, one. One single soul on his conscience, to set against all the others.

Margrethe   But that one single soul was emperor of the universe, no less than each of us. Until the morning came.

Heisenberg   No, when the morning came I persuaded them to let him go.

Bohr   Heisenberg, I have to say – if people are to be measured strictly in terms of observable quantities . . .

Heisenberg   Then we should need a strange new quantum ethics. There'd be a place in heaven for me. And another one for the SS man I met on my way home from Haigerloch. That was the end of my war. The Allied troops were closing in; there was nothing more we could do. Elisabeth and the children had taken refuge in a village in Bavaria, so I went to see them before I was captured. I had to go by bicycle – there were no trains or road transport by that time – and I had to travel by night and sleep under a hedge by day, because all through the daylight hours the skies were full of Allied planes, scouring the roads for anything that moved. A man on a bicycle would have been the biggest target left in Germany. Three days and three nights I travelled. Out of Württemberg, down through the Swabian Jura and the first foothills of the Alps. Across my ruined homeland. Was this what I'd chosen for it? This endless rubble? This perpetual smoke in the sky? These hungry faces? Was this my doing? And all the desperate people on the roads. The most desperate of all were the SS. Bands of fanatics with nothing left to lose, roaming around shooting deserters out of hand, hanging them from roadside trees. The second night, and suddenly there it is – the terrible familiar black tunic emerging from the twilight in front of me. On his lips as I stop – the one terrible familiar word. 'Deserter,' he says. He sounds as exhausted as I am. I give him the travel order I've written for myself. But there's hardly enough light in the sky to read by, and he's too weary to bother. He begins to open his holster instead. He's going to shoot me because it's simply less labour. And suddenly I'm thinking very quickly and clearly – it's like ski-ing, or that night on Heligoland, or the one in Faelled Park. What comes into my mind this time is the pack of American cigarettes I've got in my pocket. And already it's in my hand – I'm holding it out to him. The most desperate solution to a problem yet. I wait while he stands there looking at it, trying to make it out, trying to think, his left hand holding my useless piece of paper, his right on the fastening of the holster. There are two simple words in large print on the pack: Lucky Strike. He closes the holster, and takes the cigarettes instead. . . . It had worked, it had worked! Like all the other solutions to all the other problems. For twenty cigarettes he let me live. And on I went. Three days and three nights. Past the weeping children, the lost and hungry children, drafted to fight, then abandoned by their commanders. Past the starving slave-labourers walking home to France, to Poland, to Estonia. Through Gammertingen and Biberach and Memmingen. Mindelheim, Kaufbeuren, and Schöngau. Across my beloved homeland. My ruined and dishonoured and beloved homeland.

Bohr My dear Heisenberg! My dear friend!

Margrethe Silence. The silence we always in the end return to.

Heisenberg And of course I know what they're thinking about.

Margrethe All those lost children on the road.

Bohr Heisenberg wandering the world like a lost child himself.

Margrethe Our own lost children.

Heisenberg And over goes the tiller once again.

Bohr So near, so near! So slight a thing!

Margrethe He stands in the doorway, watching me, then he turns his head away . . .

Heisenberg And once again away he goes, into the dark waters.

Bohr Before we can lay our hands on anything, our life's over.

Heisenberg Before we can glimpse who or what we are, we're gone and laid to dust.

Bohr Settled among all the dust we raised.

Margrethe And sooner or later there will come a time when all our children are laid to dust, and all our children's children.

Bohr When no more decisions, great or small, are ever made again. When there's no more uncertainty, because there's no more knowledge.

Margrethe And when all our eyes are closed, when even the ghosts have gone, what will be left of our beloved world? Our ruined and dishonoured and beloved world?

Heisenberg But in the meanwhile, in this most precious meanwhile, there it is. The trees in Faelled Park. Gammertingen and Biberach and Mindelheim. Our children and our children's children. Preserved, just possibly, by that one short moment in Copenhagen. By some event that will never quite be located or defined. By that final core of uncertainty at the heart of things.

POSTSCRIPT

Where a work of fiction features historical characters and historical events it's reasonable to want to know how much of it is fiction and how much of it is history. So let me make it as clear as I can in regard to this play.

The central event in it is a real one. Heisenberg *did* go to Copenhagen in 1941, and there *was* a meeting with Bohr, in the teeth of all the difficulties encountered by my characters. He almost certainly went to dinner at the Bohrs' house, and the two men almost certainly went for a walk to escape from any possible microphones, though there is some dispute about even these simple matters. The question of what they actually said to each other has been even more disputed, and where there's ambiguity in the play about what happened, it's because there is in the recollection of the participants. Much more sustained speculation still has been devoted to the question of what Heisenberg was hoping to achieve by the meeting. All the alternative and co-existing explications offered in the play, except perhaps the final one, have been aired at various times, in one form or another.

Most anxious of all to establish some agreed version of the meeting was Heisenberg himself. He did indeed go back in 1947 with his British minder, Ronald Fraser, and attempted to find some common ground in the matter with Bohr. But it proved to be too delicate a task, and (according to Heisenberg, at any rate, in his memoirs), 'we both came to feel that it would be better to stop disturbing the spirits of the past.' This is where my play departs from the historical record, by supposing that at some later time, when everyone involved had become spirits of the past themselves, they argued the question out further, until they had achieved a little more understanding of what was going on, just as they had so many times when they were alive with the intractable difficulties presented by the internal workings of the atom.

The account of these earlier discussions in the twenties reflects at any rate one or two of the key topics, and the passion with which the argument was conducted, as it emerges from the biographical and autobiographical record.

The account of the German and American bomb programmes, and of the two physicists' participation in them, is factual; so is the fate of Danish Jewry, Heisenberg's experiences in Germany before and during the war, his subsequent internment, and the depression that clouded his later years. I have filled out some of the details, but in general what he says happened to him – at the end of the First World War, on Heligoland, during his nocturnal walk in Faelled Park, during the Berlin air raid and his internment, and on his ride across Germany, with its near-fatal encounter along the way – is based very closely upon the accounts he gave in life.

The actual words spoken by my characters are, of course, entirely their own. If this needs any justification then I can only appeal to Heisenberg himself. In his memoirs dialogue plays an important part, he says, because he hopes 'to demonstrate that science is rooted in conversations'. But, as he explains, conversations, even real conversations, cannot be reconstructed literally several decades later. So he freely reinvents them, and appeals in his turn to Thucydides. (Heisenberg's father was a professor of classics, and he was an accomplished classicist himself, on top of all his other distinctions.) Thucydides explains in his preface to the *History of the Peloponnesian War* that, although he had avoided all 'storytelling', when it came to the speeches, 'I have found it impossible to remember their exact wording. Hence I have made each orator speak as, in my opinion, he would have done in the circumstances, but keeping as close as I could to the train of thought that guided his actual speech.' Thucydides was trying to give an account of speeches that had actually been made, many of which he had himself heard. Some of the dialogue in my play represents speeches that must have been made in one form or another; some of it speeches that were certainly never made at all. I hope, though, that in some sense it respects the Thucydidean principle, and that speeches (and indeed actions) follow in so far as possible the original protagonists' train of thought.

But how far is it possible to know what their train of thought was? This is where I have departed from the established historical record – from any possible historical record. The great challenge facing the storyteller and the historian alike is to get inside people's heads, to stand where they stood and see the world as they saw it, to make some informed estimate of their motives and intentions – and this is precisely where recorded and recordable history cannot reach. Even when all the external evidence has been mastered, the only way into the protagonists' heads is through the imagination. This indeed is the substance of the play.

*

I can't claim to be the first person to notice the parallels between Heisenberg's science and his life. They provide David Cassidy with the title (*Uncertainty*) for his excellent biography (the standard work in English). 'Especially difficult and controversial,' says Cassidy in his introduction, 'is a retrospective evaluation of Heisenberg's activities during the Third Reich and particularly during World War II. Since the end of the war, an enormous range of views about this man and his behaviour have been expressed, views that have been fervently, even passionately, held by a variety of individuals. It is as if, for some, the intense emotions unleashed by the unspeakable horrors of that war and regime have combined with the many ambiguities, dualities, and compromises of Heisenberg's life and actions to make Heisenberg himself subject to a type of uncertainty principle . . .' Thomas Powers makes a similar point in his extraordinary and encyclopaedic book *Heisenberg's War*, which first aroused my interest in the trip to Copenhagen; he says that Heisenberg's later reticence on his role in the failure of the German bomb programme 'introduces an element of irreducible uncertainty'.

Cassidy does not explore the parallel further. Powers even appends a footnote to his comment: 'Forgive me.' The apology seems to me unnecessary. It's true that the concept of uncertainty is one of those scientific notions that has become common coinage, and generalised to the point of

losing much of its original meaning. The idea as introduced
by Heisenberg into quantum mechanics was precise and
technical. It didn't suggest that everything about the
behaviour of particles was unknowable, or hazy. What it
limited was the simultaneous measurement of 'canonically
conjugate variables', such as position and momentum, or
energy and time. The more precisely you measure one
variable, it said, the less precise your measurement of the
related variable can be; and this ratio, the uncertainty
relationship, is itself precisely formulable.

None of this, plainly, applies directly to our observations
of thought and intention. Thoughts are not locatable by pairs
of conjugate variables, so there can be no question of a ratio
of precision. Powers seems to imply that in Heisenberg's case
the uncertainty arises purely because 'questions of motive
and intention cannot be established more clearly than he was
willing to state them'. It's true that Heisenberg was under
contradictory pressures after the war which made it
particularly difficult for him to explain what he had been
trying to do. He wanted to distance himself from the Nazis,
but he didn't want to suggest that he had been a traitor. He
was reluctant to claim to his fellow-Germans that he had
deliberately lost them the war, but he was no less reluctant
to suggest that he had failed them simply out of
incompetence.

But the uncertainty surely begins long before the point
where Heisenberg might have offered an explanation. He
was under at least as many contradictory pressures at the
time to shape the actions he later failed to explain, and the
uncertainty would still have existed, for us and for him, even
if he had been as open, honest, and helpful as it is humanly
possible to be. What people say about their own motives and
intentions, even when they are not caught in the traps that
entangled Heisenberg, is always subject to question – as
subject to question as what anybody else says about them.
Thoughts and intentions, even one's own – perhaps one's
own most of all – remain shifting and elusive. There is not
one single thought or intention of any sort that can ever be
precisely established.

What the uncertainty of thoughts does have in common with the uncertainty of particles is that the difficulty is not just a practical one, but a systematic limitation which cannot even in theory be circumvented. It is patently not resolved by the efforts of psychologists and psychoanalysts, and it will not be resolved by neurologists either, even when everything is known about the structure and workings of the brain, any more than semantic questions can be resolved by looking at the machine code of a computer. And since, as the Copenhagen Interpretation establishes, the whole possibility of saying or thinking anything about the world, even the most apparently objective, abstract aspects of it studied by the natural sciences, depends upon human observation, and is subject to the limitations which the human mind imposes, this uncertainty in our thinking is also fundamental to the nature of the world.

'Uncertainty' is not a very satisfactory word to come at this. It sits awkwardly even in its original context. You can be uncertain about things which are themselves entirely definite, and about which you could be entirely certain if you were simply better informed. Indeed, the very idea of uncertainty seems to imply the possibility of certainty. Heisenberg and Bohr used several different German words in different contexts. Bohr (who spoke more or less perfect German) sometimes referred to *Unsicherheit*, which means quite simply, unsureness. In Heisenberg's original paper he talks about *Ungenauigkeit* – inexactness. But the word he adopts in his general conclusion, and which he uses when he refers back to the period later in his memoirs, is *Unbestimmtheit*, for which it's harder to find a satisfactory English equivalent. Although it means uncertainty in the sense of vagueness, it's plainly derived from *bestimmen*, to determine or to ascertain. This is reflected better in the other English translation which is sometimes used, but which seems to be less familiar, indeterminacy. 'Undeterminedness' would be closer still, though clumsy. Less close to the German, but even closer to the reality of the situation, would be 'indeterminability'.

Questions of translation apart, Heisenberg's choice of

word suggests that, at the time he wrote his paper, he had
not fully grasped the metaphysical implications of what he
was saying. Indeed, he concludes that the experiments
concerned are affected by *Unbestimmtheit* 'purely empirically'.
He was not, as Bohr complained, at that time greatly
interested in the philosophical fall-out from physics and
mathematics (though he became much more so later on in
life), and he was publishing in a hurry, as Bohr also
complained, before he had had a chance to discuss the work
with either Bohr or anyone else. His paper seems to imply
that electrons have definite orbits, even if these are
unknowable; he talks about a quantum of light completely
throwing the electron out of its 'orbit', even though he puts
the word into inverted commas, and says that it has no
rational sense here. The title of the paper itself reinforces this
impression: *Über den anschaulichen Inhalt der quantentheoretischen
Kinematik und Mechanik*. Again there are translation problems.
'*Anschaulich*' means graphic, concrete, 'look-at-able'; the title
is usually translated as referring to the 'perceptual' content of
the disciplines concerned, which again seems to suggest a
contrast with their unperceived aspects – as if Heisenberg
were concerned merely about our difficulties in visualising
abstractions, not about the physical implications of this.

*

What about my characters? Are they anything like their
originals?

It's impossible to catch the exact tone of voice of people
one never knew, with only the written record to go on,
especially when most of what their contemporaries recall
them as saying was originally said in other languages. There
are particular problems with all three of my protagonists.
Bohr was as notorious for his inarticulacy and inaudibility as
he was famous for his goodness and lovability. Weizsäcker
writes about Bohr's 'helplessly amiable way of talking'.
Schrödinger, after his epic confrontation with Bohr in 1926,
described him as often talking 'for minutes almost in a
dreamlike, visionary and really quite unclear manner, partly

because he is so full of consideration and constantly hesitates
– fearing that the other might take a statement of his
[Bohr's] point of view as an insufficient appreciation of the
other's . . .' My Bohr is necessarily a little more coherent
than this.

The problem with Margrethe is that there is relatively
little biographical material to go on. She and Niels were
plainly mutually devoted, and everything suggests that she
was as generally loved as he was. She had no scientific
training, but Bohr constantly discussed his work with her,
presumably avoiding technical language – though she must
have become fairly familiar with even that, since she typed
out each draft of his papers. I suspect she was more gracious
and reserved than she appears here, but she plainly had
great firmness of character – in later life she was known as
Dronning (Queen) Margrethe. She was always cooler about
Heisenberg than Bohr was, and she was openly angry about
his visit in 1941. According to Bohr she objected strongly to
his being invited to the house, and relented only when Bohr
promised to avoid politics and restrict the conversation to
physics. Bohr himself always refused to be drawn about
Heisenberg's trip in 1941, but she insisted, even after the
war, even after all Heisenberg's attempts to explain, 'No
matter what anyone says, that was a hostile visit.'

The problem with Heisenberg is his elusiveness and
ambiguity, which is of course what the play is about. The
one thing that everyone agreed upon about him was what
Max Born, his mentor in Göttingen, called 'his unbelievable
quickness and precision of understanding'. The contrast with
Bohr is almost comic. 'Probably [Bohr's] most characteristic
property,' according to George Gamow, 'was the slowness of
his thinking and comprehension.'

As a young man Heisenberg seems to have had an
appealing eagerness and directness. Born described him as
looking like a simple farm boy, with clear bright eyes, and a
radiant expression on his face. Somebody else thought he
looked 'like a bright carpenter's apprentice just returned
from technical school'. Victor Weisskopf says that he made
friends easily, and that everyone liked him. Bohr, after their

first meeting in 1922, was delighted by Heisenberg's 'nice shy nature, his good temper, his eagerness and his enthusiasm'. There was something about him of the prize-winning student, who is good at everything required of him, and Bohr was not the only father-figure to whom he appealed. He had a somewhat similar relationship to Sommerfeld, his first professor in Munich, and in his difficulties with the Nazis he turned to two elders of German physics for counsel, Max Planck and Max von Laue. His closest friend and colleague was probably Carl Friedrich von Weizsäcker, who was younger than him, but it is striking that during his internment the person he chose to confide his explanation of the Hiroshima bomb to was not Weizsäcker, who was interned with him, but the 66-year-old Otto Hahn.

Margrethe always found him difficult, closed, and oversensitive, and this propensity to be withdrawn and inturned was exacerbated as life went on – first by his political problems in the thirties, and then by his efforts to reconcile the moral irreconcilables of his wartime work. His autobiographical writing is rather stiff and formal, and his letters to Bohr, even during the twenties and thirties, are correct rather than intimate. Throughout the period of their closest friendship they addressed each other with the formal *Sie*, and switched to *du* only when Heisenberg also had a chair.

The conversations that Heisenberg claimed such freedom to recreate in his memoirs are stately. Much more plausibly colloquial is the transcript of David Irving's long interview with him for *The Virus House*, Irving's history of the German bomb programme, though he is still (naturally) watchful. In the transcripts of the relatively unguarded conversations that the German atomic team had among themselves during their internment, where Heisenberg emerges as the dominant figure, both morally and practically, a certain hard-headed worldlinesss can be detected. When one of the others says that if they agree to work on atomic matters under Allied control they will be looked down upon as traitors 'in the eyes of the masses', Heisenberg replies: 'No. One must do that cleverly. As far as the masses are concerned it will look as though we unfortunately have to continue our scientific work under the wicked Anglo-Saxon control, and that we can do nothing about it. We will have to appear to accept this control with fury and gnashing of teeth.'

There was always something a little sharp and harsh about him, something that at its best inspired respect rather than love, and that after the war occasioned really quite astonishing hostility and contempt. Even Samuel Goudsmit turned against him. Goudsmit was an old friend and colleague; when the investigators of the Alsos mission, the Allied agency for gathering intelligence on German atomic research, for which he was working, finally broke into Heisenberg's office in 1945, one of the first things they saw was a picture of the two of them together that Heisenberg had kept there as a memento of happier days. But when Goudsmit subsequently interrogated Heisenberg he found him arrogant and self-involved. Goudsmit had understandably bitter feelings at the time – he had just discovered the record of his parents' death in Auschwitz. Heisenberg was also caught in a false position. Confident that his team had been far ahead of the Americans, he offered Goudsmit his services in initiating them into the secrets of uranium fission. (Goudsmit did nothing to correct his misapprehension, which gave Heisenberg, when the truth finally came out, grounds for returning Goudsmit's bitterness.) In his superficial and strangely unimpressive book on Alsos, Goudsmit wrote about Heisenberg and his team with contemptuous dismissal, and in the year-long correspondence in the American press that followed its publication, accused him of self-importance and dishonesty.

Weisskopf gave a reception for Heisenberg during his trip to America in 1949, but about half the guests – including many people from the Los Alamos team – failed to appear, explaining to Weisskopf that they didn't want to shake the hand of the man who had tried to build a bomb for Hitler. Ronald Fraser, the British intelligence officer who escorted Heisenberg back to Copenhagen in 1947 (the British seem to have been frightened that he would defect to the Russians, or be kidnapped by them) replied to Irving's inquiry about

the trip in tones of patronising contempt that seem slightly
unhinged. 'The whole story of "a kind of confrontation",' he
wrote to Irving, 'in the matter of his 1941 natter with Bohr
in the Tivoli Gardens [*sic*] is a typical Heisenberg fabrication
– maybe a bit brighter than a thousand others, but like them
all a product of his *Blut und Boden* guilt complex, which he
rationalises that quickly that the stories become *for him* the
truth, the whole truth, and nothing but the truth. Pitiful, in a
man of his mental stature.'

Goudsmit gradually modified his opinion, and his final
judgment on Heisenberg, when he died in 1976, was a
generous one which goes some way to expunging the
dismissive tone of his book: 'Heisenberg was a very great
physicist, a deep thinker, a fine human being, and also a
courageous person. He was one of the greatest physicists of
our time, but he suffered severely under the unwarranted
attacks by fanatical colleagues. In my opinion he must be
considered to have been in some respects a victim of the
Nazi regime.'

But others have continued to take a high moral tone (cf
the historian Professor Rose, in a paper written as late as
1984, entitled *Heisenberg, German Morality and the Atomic Bomb*:
'. . . guff . . . self-serving, self-deluding claims . . . elementary
moral stupidity . . .') Gitta Sereny, in her new book *Albert
Speer: His Battle with Truth*, continues the tradition, and
dismisses Heisenberg's account of his intentions as simply
false.[1] Even Cassidy, who gives full measure to Heisenberg

[1] Her arguments are extremely difficult to make any sense of. Speer had written in
his memoirs that he was 'rather put out' by the very small amount of money that
Heisenberg, after their meeting in 1942, requested to run the nuclear research
programme. In Speer's 'Spandau draft' of the manuscript, says Sereny, he 'adds in
brackets a remark he did *not* use in his book: "I do hope Heisenberg is not now
claiming that they tried, for reasons of principle, to sabotage the project by asking for
such minimal support!"' Heisenberg, she says, 'did in fact try precisely that after the
war,' but doesn't say where or when he tried it. So far as I know he waited until this
year, when he at last mentioned the matter posthumously and fictitiously in my play.
The only references to the smallness of the sums of money he asked for that I can
find in the record are by Speer himself, and by Field Marshal Milch, Goering's
deputy in the Luftwaffe, who was also present at the meeting; there's certainly
nothing about it in Heisenberg's memoirs, or in his long interview with Irving.

Sereny goes on to argue that Heisenberg's claims about his intentions in meeting
Bohr in 1941 'are now shown by Speer's Spandau account to be false', though quite

as a physicist in his biography, published in 1992, is notably
cool and cautious in his assessment of Heisenberg's role in
the German bomb programme. For a really spirited and
thoroughly researched defence of Heisenberg one has to turn
to Powers' book, published the following year. It is a
remarkable piece of work, journalistic in tone, but huge in its
scope and generous in its understanding. If it has a fault it is
Powers' inability to resist being side-tracked from the main
narrative by the amazing byways that he perpetually finds
opening off it. I recommend it particularly to other
dramatists and screenwriters; there is material here for
several more plays and films yet.

Powers' argument is that the Allied bomb programme
succeeded because of the uninhibited eagerness of the
scientists to do it, particularly of those exiles who had known
Nazism at first hand, and who were desperate to pre-empt
Hitler; while the German programme failed because of the
underlying reluctance of scientists in Germany to arm Hitler
with the bomb, however strong their patriotism, and
however much they wanted to profit from the possibilities for
research. 'Zeal was needed,' he says; 'its absence was lethal,
like a poison that leaves no trace.'

But he goes further, and argues that Heisenberg 'did not

how this is so she doesn't explain. About what she calls 'the facts' of the Copenhagen
meeting she is remarkably brisk. In the conversation '. . . which Bohr subsequently
reported to his associates at the Niels Bohr Institute, Heisenberg had made his
political stand crystal clear. His team, he told Bohr, had gone some way towards
discovering a way to produce an atom bomb. Germany was going to win the war,
probably quite soon, and Bohr should join them now in their efforts.'

The only reference that Sereny gives for her account of the Copenhagen meeting is
Powers' *Heisenberg's War*, and the only authority in Powers (or anywhere else, so far as
I know) for the view that Heisenberg was inviting Bohr to work on the German
bomb (surely the least plausible out of all the various readings on offer, completely at
odds with what Weisskopf recalls Bohr as saying in 1948, and with what Bohr is on
record as telling Chadwick at the time) is some person or persons unnamed in
Copenhagen who 44 years later told Weizsäcker (who told Powers) that this is what
Bohr had said he had believed Heisenberg's intention to be. Even if it really is what
Bohr believed, it is of course not what Weizsäcker believed, or Powers either. They
are reporting Bohr's alleged belief as a possible misapprehension on his part which
might have explained his anger. Indeed, Powers' own reading of the situation is
precisely the one that Sereny claims to be discredited by Speer's remark. In any case,
the suggestion that Heisenberg thought he might be able to import someone half-
Jewish into the most secret research programme in Nazi Germany is frankly
preposterous.

simply withhold himself, stand aside, let the project die. He killed it.' He tries to show that at every point Heisenberg was careful to hold out enough hope to the authorities to ensure that he and and his team were left in charge of the project, but never enough to attract the total commitment and huge investment that would have offered the only real hope of success. 'Heisenberg's caution saved him. He was free to do what he could to guide the German atomic research effort into a broom closet, where scientists tinkered until the war ended.'

The play is not an attempt to adjudicate between these differing views of Heisenberg. It must be noted, however, that Powers has the advantage of access to one crucial piece of evidence that was denied to Cassidy, and to almost everyone who wrote on Heisenberg earlier – the transcripts of the Farm Hall recordings.

*

The story of Farm Hall is another complete play in itself. (Sir Charles Frank, the British atomic physicist, in his admirably fair and clear introduction to the published text of the transcripts, regrets that they were not released in time for Dürrenmatt to make use of.)

At the end of the war troops of the Alsos mission, to which Goudsmit was attached, made their way through what was left of the German front line and located the remains of the German reactor at Haigerloch, with the intention of finally reassuring themselves that Germany would not be able to spring some terrible nuclear surprise at the last moment. They also seized the team of scientists themselves, making a special armed sortie to Urfeld, in Bavaria, to collect Heisenberg from his home. Haigerloch and Hechingen, the nearby town where the team was based, were in the French sector. The scientists were abstracted secretly, from under the noses of the French, and brought back to Britain, where they were held, illicitly and without anyone's knowledge, in a former Intelligence safe house – Farm Hall, near Cambridge. The intention seems to have

been partly to prevent their passing on any atomic secrets to
either of our other two allies, the Russians and the French;
partly to forestall any discussion of the possibility of nuclear
weapons until we had completed and used our own; and
partly, perhaps, to save Heisenberg and the others from the
alternative solution to these problems proposed by one
American general, which was simply to shoot them out of
hand.

They were detained at Farm Hall for six months, during
which time they were treated not as prisoners but as guests.
Hidden microphones, however, had been installed, and
everything they said to each other was secretly recorded.
The existence of the transcripts from these recordings was
kept as secret as that of the prisoners. General Groves, the
head of the Allied bomb programme, quoted from them in
his memoirs (1962), and Goudsmit plainly had access to
them, which he drew upon in his book on Alsos, but the
British Government, in a particularly irrational manifestation
of its usual pathological addiction to secrecy, continued to
block the release of the papers themselves. Even Margaret
Gowing was refused access when she wrote her official
history of British atomic policy in 1964, and David Irving
was refused again, in spite of strenuous efforts, for *The Virus
House* in 1967. The ban was maintained until 1992, when the
Government finally gave way to a combined appeal from
leading scientists and historians.

The German originals are lost, and the translation was
plainly done under pressure, with little feeling for colloquial
nuance, but the transcripts are direct evidence of what
Heisenberg and the others thought when they were talking,
as they believed, amongst themselves. They are particularly
revealing in the moment of unguarded horror that followed
the announcement of Hiroshima. The conversations reflect a
great range of attitudes, but in general seem to me to
support the idea that for all practical purposes German
thinking had stopped at a reactor, and that there had been
no eagerness at all to look beyond this to the possibility of
weapons. 'I was absolutely convinced,' says Heisenberg at
one point in that long and anguished night, 'of the possibility

of our making an uranium engine [reactor] but I never
thought that we would make a bomb and at the bottom of
my heart I was really glad that it was to be an engine and
not a bomb. I must admit that.' Weizsäcker says that he
doesn't think that they should make excuses now for failing,
'but we must admit that we didn't want to succeed.' Wirtz:
'One cannot say in front of an Englishman that we didn't try
hard enough. They were our enemies, although we
sabotaged the war. There are some things that one knows
and one can discuss together but that one cannot discuss in
the presence of Englishmen.'

Even if you discount all this as *post hoc* rationalisation for
failure, the published text casts grave doubt on the use that
Goudsmit seems to have made of the transcripts, to support
his view, shared by Rose, that the Germans failed because
they thought of the bomb as a kind of reactor, using slow
neutrons in U-238. What Heisenberg tells Hahn that same
night, when Gerlach, their Nazi co-ordinator, has retired to
sob in his room, and they are finally alone together, is that
'quite honestly I have never worked it out as I never
believed one could get pure 235. I always knew it could be
done with 235 with fast neutrons. That's why 235 only
[presumably = "only 235"] can be used as an explosive.
One can never make an explosive with slow neutrons, not
even with the heavy water machine [the German reactor], as
then the neutrons only go with thermal speed, with the result
that the reaction is so slow that the thing explodes sooner,
before the reaction is complete.' He went on to suggest that
the critical mass could have been drastically reduced by the
use of a reflector to cut down neutron escape.

The exact time of this conversation is not given. The
internees had been told about Hiroshima by their (almost)
endlessly sympathetic and urbane gaoler-cum-host, Major
Rittner, at dinner-time, and Heisenberg had not believed it
until he had heard it with his own ears on the BBC nine
o'clock news. It plainly took place within a matter of hours –
hours which seem to have been spent entirely in stunned
discussion with the others, without any chance for further
thought or work on the problem.

A week later, admittedly with the help of what few details the newspapers had given of the two bombs, Heisenberg offered all his fellow-internees a lecture in which he presented a complete and considered account of how the Allies had done it. At the end of the lecture, says Powers, 'the German scientists, given a second chance, would have been ready to start building a bomb.' But, as Powers adds, the inclusion in the lecture of quite fundamental matters, together with the questions which his hearers asked, make it clear that it was all news to everyone present except his closest associates. 'What the Farm Hall transcripts show unmistakably is that Heisenberg did not explain basic bomb physics to the man in charge of the German bomb program [Gerlach] until after the war was over.' They 'offer strong evidence that Heisenberg never explained fast fission to Gerlach, that he cooked up a plausible method of estimating critical mass which gave an answer in tons, and that he well knew how to make a bomb with far less, but kept the knowledge to himself'.

I don't think I'm quite convinced by the idea that Heisenberg had cooked something up. It's true that he had kept his evident knowledge of the reflector to himself, together with the drastic reduction in the demand for fissile material that this offered. But I can't see why he should have wanted to conceal any deliberate fabrication from Hahn, on the night of Hiroshima, and I'm rather inclined to trust his 'quite honestly' when he tells Hahn that he'd never worked out the diffusion equation for pure 235 because he'd never believed that pure 235 would be available. In my view it's more likely that he had kept the knowledge of how fast the reaction would go in pure 235, and therefore of how little of it would be needed, not to himself but from himself.

In the end, it seems to me, your judgment of Heisenberg comes down to what you make of his failure to attempt this fundamental calculation. Incompetence, arrogance, stupidity, as his detractors have claimed? It's possible. Even the greatest scientists – and Heisenberg was undoubtedly one of them – make mistakes, and fail to see possibilities that lesser men pick up; Heisenberg accepted that he had made a mistake in the formulation of uncertainty itself. Or was there an unconscious reluctance to challenge such a comforting and convenient assumption? Comforting and convenient, that is, if what he was trying to do was *not* to build a bomb. Is it all part of a general pattern of reluctance, as Powers suggests? Is this supported by the vigorous, and successful, campaign he fought in the 1950s, together with Weizsäcker and others, to defeat the proposal to arm even the constitutional Germany of the Federal Republic with nuclear weapons?

There is one small piece of evidence, curiously not mustered by Powers, which seems worth mentioning: the question of the cyclotron. At the crucial meeting between Heisenberg and Speer in 1942, which seems finally to have scuppered all possibility of a German bomb, Heisenberg is reported to have emphasised the need to build a cyclotron. A cyclotron could have been used, as the cyclotrons in America were, for isotope separation, the great sticking-point in the German programme. In the account of this meeting in his memoirs Speer says: 'Difficulties were compounded, Heisenberg explained, by the fact that Europe possessed only one cyclotron, and that of minimal capacity. Moreover, it was located in Paris and because of the need for secrecy could not be used to full advantage.' Powers mentions this, but does not go on to the obvious corollary: that if Speer's recollection is accurate, then Heisenberg was plainly lying, because he knew perfectly well that there was a second cyclotron to hand – at Bohr's institute in Copenhagen. This would suggest that his apparent anxiety to lay his hands on a machine that might actually separate some U-235 was not quite what it seemed. Or, at the very least, that he placed Germany's war aims below his desire to protect Bohr's institute. Perhaps Speer is simply wrong. It seems uncharacteristic of Heisenberg to have risked such a blatant falsehood, and he makes no mention of it in his own accounts of the meeting. All the same, when he went back to Copenhagen in 1944, after Bohr had fled, to adjudicate a German proposal to strip the institute of all its equipment, presumably including the cyclotron, he seems to have contrived to leave it even then still in Danish hands.

*

One looming imponderable remains. *If* Heisenberg had
made the calculation, and *if* the resulting reduction in the
scale of the problem had somehow generated a real
eagerness in both the Nazi authorities and the scientists,
could the Germans have built a bomb? Frank believes that
they could not have done it before the war in Europe was
over – 'even the Americans, with substantial industrial and
scientific advantage, and the important assistance from
Britain and from ex-Germans in Britain did not achieve that
(VE-Day, 8 May 1945, Trinity test, Alamogordo, 6 July
1945).' Speer (who as armaments minister would presumably
have had to carry the programme out) suggests in his
memoirs that it might have been possible to do it by 1945, if
the Germans had shelved all their other weapons projects,
then two paragraphs later more cautiously changes his
estimate to 1947; but of course he needs to justify his failure
to pursue the possibility. Powers makes the point that,
whatever the timetable was, its start date could have been
much earlier. Atomic energy in Germany, he argues,
attracted the interest of the authorities from the first day of
the war. 'The United States, beginning in June 1942, took
just over three years to do the job, and the Soviet Union
succeeded in four. If a serious effort to develop a bomb had
commenced in mid-1940, one might have been tested in
1943, well before the Allied bomber offensive had destroyed
German industry.'

If this 'serious effort' had begun only after Heisenberg's
visit to Copenhagen, as the play suggests might have
happened if the conversation with Bohr had gone differently,
then even this timetable wouldn't have delivered a bomb
until late 1944 – and by that time it was of course much less
likely that German industry could have delivered. In any
case, formidable difficulties would have had to be overcome
to make this possible. The German team were hugely
frustrated by their inability to find a successful method for

isolating U-235 in any appreciable quantity, even though the experimental method, using Clusius-Dickel tubes, was of German origin. They could have tried one of the processes used sucessfully by the Allies, gaseous diffusion. This was another German method, developed in Berlin by Gustav Hertz, but Hertz had lost his job because his uncle was Jewish. (It was, incidentally, the delays in getting the various American isotope-separation plants to function which meant that the Allied bomb was not ready in time for use against Germany.)

The failure to separate 235 also held up the reactor programme, and therefore the prospect of producing plutonium, because they could not separate enough of it even for the purposes of enrichment (increasing the 235 content of natural uranium), so that it was harder to get the reactor to go critical. The construction of the reactor was further delayed because Walther Bothe's team at Heidelberg estimated the neutron absorption rates of graphite wrongly, which obliged the designers to use heavy water as a moderator instead. The only source of heavy water was a plant in Norway, which was forced to close after a series of attacks by Norwegian parachutists attached to Special Operations Executive, American bombers, and the Norwegian Resistance. Though perhaps, if a crash programme had been instituted from the first day of the war, enough heavy water might have been accumulated before the attacks were mounted.

If, if, if. . . . The line of ifs is a long one. It remains just possible, though. The effects of real enthusiasm and real determination are incalculable. In the realm of the just possible they are sometimes decisive.

*

Anyone interested enough in any of these questions to want to sidestep the fiction and look at the historical record should certainly begin with:

Thomas Powers, *Heisenberg's War* (Cape, 1993)

David Cassidy, *Uncertainty: The Life and Science of Werner Heisenberg* (Freedman, 1992)

Abraham Pais, *Niels Bohr's Times* (OUP, 1991) – Pais is a fellow nuclear physicist, who knew Bohr personally, and this, in its highly eccentric way, is a classic of biography, even though Pais has not much more sense of narrative than I have of physics, and the book is organised more like a scientific report than the story of someone's life. But then Bohr notoriously had no sense of narrative, either. One of the tasks his assistants had was to take him to the cinema and to explain the plot to him afterwards.

Werner Heisenberg, *Physics and Beyond* (Harper & Row, 1971) – In German, *Der Teil und das Ganze*. His memoirs.

Operation Epsilon, the Farm Hall Transcripts, introduced by Sir Charles Frank. (Institute of Physics Publishing, 1993)

Also relevant:

Heisenberg, *Physics and Philosophy* (Penguin, 1958)

Niels Bohr, *The Philosophical Writings of Niels Bohr* (Oxbow Press, 1987)

Elizabeth Heisenberg, *Inner Exile* (Birkhauser, 1984) – In German, *Das politische Leben eines Unpolitischen*. Defensive in tone, but revealing about the kind of anguish her husband tended to conceal from the world; and the source for Heisenberg's ride home in 1945.

David Irving, *The Virus House* (Collins, 1967). The story of the German bomb programme.

Records and Documents Relating to the Third Reich, II German Atomic Research, Microfilms DJ29–32 (EP Microform Ltd, Wakefield). Irving's research materials for the book, including long verbatim interviews with Heisenberg and others. The only consultable copy I could track down was in the library of the Ministry of Defence.

Archive for the History of Quantum Physics, microfilm. Includes the complete correspondence of Heisenberg and Bohr. A copy is available for reference in the Science Museum Library. Bohr's side of the correspondence is almost entirely in Danish, Heisenberg's in German, apart from one letter.

Leni Yahil, *The Rescue of Danish Jewry* (1969)

There are also many interesting sidelights on life at the Bohr Institute in its golden years in:

French & Kennedy, eds., *Niels Bohr, A Centenary Volume* (1985)

and in the memoirs of Hendrik Casimir, George Gamow, Otto Frisch, Otto Hahn, Rudolf Peierls, and Victor Weisskopf.

A SELECTED LIST OF
METHUEN MODERN PLAYS

• All Methuen Drama books are available through mail order or from your local bookshop.

Please send cheque/eurocheque/postal order (sterling only) Access, Visa, Mastercard, Diners Card, Switch or Amex.

☐☐☐☐☐☐☐☐☐☐☐☐☐☐

Expiry Date:_____ Signature: _____

Please allow 75 pence per book for post and packing U.K.
Overseas customers please allow £1.00 per copy for post and packing.

ALL ORDERS TO:

Methuen Books, Books by Post, TBS Limited, The Book Service, Colchester Road, Frating Green, Colchester, Essex CO7 7DW.

NAME: _____

ADDRESS: _____

_____

_____

Please allow 28 days for delivery. Please tick box if you do not
wish to receive any additional information   ☐

Prices and availability subject to change without notice.

Methuen Contemporary Dramatists
include

Peter Barnes (three volumes)
Sebastian Barry
Edward Bond (six volumes)
Howard Brenton
  (two volumes)
Richard Cameron
Jim Cartwright
Caryl Churchill (two volumes)
Sarah Daniels (two volumes)
David Edgar (three volumes)
Dario Fo (two volumes)
Michael Frayn (two volumes)
Peter Handke
Jonathan Harvey
Declan Hughes
Terry Johnson
Bernard-Marie Koltès
Doug Lucie
David Mamet (three volumes)

Anthony Minghella
  (two volumes)
Tom Murphy (four volumes)
Phyllis Nagy
Peter Nichols (two volumes)
Philip Osment
Louise Page
Stephen Poliakoff
  (three volumes)
Christina Reid
Philip Ridley
Willy Russell
Ntozake Shange
Sam Shepard (two volumes)
David Storey (three volumes)
Sue Townsend
Michel Vinaver (two volumes)
Michael Wilcox

Methuen World Classics
include

Jean Anouilh (two volumes)
John Arden (two volumes)
Arden & D'Arcy
Brendan Behan
Aphra Behn
Bertolt Brecht (six volumes)
Büchner
Bulgakov
Calderón
Anton Chekhov
Noël Coward (five volumes)
Eduardo De Filippo
Max Frisch
Gorky
Harley Granville Barker
(two volumes)
Henrik Ibsen (six volumes)
Lorca (three volumes)
Marivaux

Mustapha Matura
David Mercer (two volumes)
Arthur Miller (five volumes)
Molière
Musset
Clifford Odets
Joe Orton
A. W. Pinero
Luigi Pirandello
Terence Rattigan
W. Somerset Maugham
(two volumes)
Wole Soyinka
August Strindberg
(three volumes)
J. M. Synge
Ramón del Valle-Inclán
Frank Wedekind
Oscar Wilde